Eric Redmond's book is one that
African American church cultur[...]
celebration in preaching is a style [...]
in media and betrayed humorously in movies. Nevertheless, at the same time
this experience has lifted up a nation and a people from the ashes of the despair.
Redmond's book will bring a sense of understanding and clarity to these experiences
and why this unique style is still beneficial in today's church.

**A.B. VINES SR.**
Bishop, New Season Global Network
Former 1st Vice President of SBC
Senior Pastor, New Seasons Church

*Say It!* provides insight and examples of how the preacher can be equally effective
in reflecting upon the human condition while at the same time skillfully applying
accurate biblical perspective and interpretation through the discipline of expository
preaching. Through its collection of expository sermons that are enveloped in the
African American preaching style, *Say It!* not only affirms the African American
preaching tradition but also and most importantly the African American preacher.
It masterfully demonstrates to the broader faith community and beyond that
the African American preacher in many instances has both the learning and the
burning. We congratulate Redmond and the faithful exegetes who have contributed
to this marvelous work on a job well done.

**KEITH W. BYRD SR.**
Second Vice President, Progressive National Baptist Convention, Inc.

In *Say It!*, Eric C. Redmond and his cowriters have produced a must-read for
students, teachers, pastors, and theologians alike. This is a highly commendable
presentation that includes practical Old and New Testament sermonic examples
of how biblical exposition can offer an effective method for powerful preaching in
the black tradition. Readers will find this work to be a proven tool and a powerful
resource.

**FELIX G. WILLIAMS III**
President, Congress of Christian Education
Progressive National Baptist Convention, Inc.
USA and International

With several illustrations of biblical expository preaching in the black tradition
included in this volume, the authors have made a clear distinction between
expository preaching in the black experience as compared to the white evangelical
tradition. Though both approaches are legitimate preaching styles, our historical
experience as African Americans making our preaching unique in style and content.
Every serious preacher will want to read this outstanding volume. It is sure to
sharpen your own preaching gifts.

**JAMES C. PERKINS**
Pastor, The Greater Christ Baptist Church, Detroit, MI
Former President, Progressive National Baptist Convention, Inc.

For the past decade or so, my own growth in preaching stems largely from sitting at the feet of expositors in this country who *Say It!* from the black tradition. My hope is that this book, long overdue, and the men who contributed chapters to it, will fill you with fresh conviction to make progress in your own preaching.

DAVID HELM
Lead Pastor, Holy Trinity Church, Hyde Park
Chairman, The Charles Simeon Trust

*Say It!* is a refreshing volume featuring twelve able practitioners in the African American preaching tradition. But the volume is far more than a book of sermons. It elucidates on principles of hermeneutics, exegesis, and especially application of truth for our generation when the excellence of the preached Word is sometimes sacrificed to satisfy the audience. The review of black preaching through the years of slavery, Jim Crow, and Civil Rights shows how God has used black ministers of the gospel to give encouragement and hope through many difficult days. The book includes a chapter encouraging preaching through the Bible with suggestions on how to do it. Both new and seasoned preachers will find the volume inspirational and instructive.

MELVIN BANKS
Founder and chairman of Urban Ministries, Inc.

As I travel the globe and sit under biblical preaching among the nations, I marvel at how God richly displays his creativity through His people. When I return home, I'm likewise privileged to hear the familiar cadence and content of my African American heritage, through the solid biblical preaching of my local pastor. *Say It!* opens doors into the exposition and style of this African American tradition for the world to explore and learn about this rich tradition from the inside out.

K. A. ELLIS
Director of the Center for the Study of the Bible and Ethnicity, RTS Atlanta

Rightly dividing the Word of truth, preaching with prophetic power, expounding the riches of God's inerrant Book—these aren't the priorities and passions of the white evangelical preacher solely. Indeed, there is a substantive and celebrated African American tradition of expository preaching that courses through the veins of church history. And now, this timely volume of essays and exemplary sermons puts this rich tradition within the grasp of a whole new generation of preachers—red and yellow, black and white. Thank you to Eric C. Redmond and his outstanding team of contributors. I can't commend this volume highly enough. Say it, brothers, and say it again!

TODD WILSON
President, The Center For Pastor Theologians

# SAY IT!

## Celebrating Expository Preaching in the African American Tradition

**General Editor**
**ERIC C. REDMOND**

MOODY PUBLISHERS

CHICAGO

All Scripture quotations, unless otherwise indicated, are taken from the Holy Bible, New International Version®, NIV®. Copyright © 1973, 1978, 1984, 2011 by Biblica, Inc.™ Used by permission of Zondervan. All rights reserved worldwide. www.zondervan.com. The "NIV" and "New International Version" are trademarks registered in the United States Patent and Trademark Office by Biblica, Inc.™

Scripture quotations marked ESV are from The Holy Bible, English Standard Version® (ESV®), copyright © 2001 by Crossway, a publishing ministry of Good News Publishers. Used by permission. All rights reserved.

Scripture quotations marked NASB are taken from the New American Standard Bible®, Copyright © 1960, 1962, 1963, 1968, 1971, 1972, 1973, 1975, 1977, 1995 by The Lockman Foundation. Used by permission. (www.Lockman.org)

Scripture quotations marked CSB are from the Christian Standard Bible®, Copyright © 2017 by Holman Bible Publishers. Used by permission. Christian Standard Bible® and CSB® are federally registered trademarks of Holman Bible Publishers.

Scripture quotations marked KJV are taken from the King James Version.

Names and details of some stories have been changed to protect the privacy of individuals.

Moody Publishers Editor: Kevin P. Emmert
Interior Design: Ragont Design
Cover Design: Charles Brock
Cover illustration of background texture copyright © 2012 by Ekely / iStock (163736108).
Cover photo of Bible page copyright © 2019 by BillionPhotos.com / Adobe Stock (87703264).
All rights reserved for all of the above photos.

All websites and phone numbers listed herein are accurate at the time of publication but may change in the future or cease to exist. The listing of website references and resources does not imply publisher endorsement of the site's entire contents. Groups and organizations are listed for informational purposes, and listing does not imply publisher endorsement of their activities.

Library of Congress Cataloging-in-Publication Data

Names: Redmond, Eric C., editor.
Title: Say it! : biblical exposition in the African American tradition /
  Eric C. Redmond, general editor
Description: Chicago : Moody Publishers, 2020. | Includes bibliographical
  references. | Summary: "Expository preaching and African American style
  are partners, not enemies. This important and powerful resource
  celebrates the faithful, biblical preaching of African Americans that is
  so often overlooked because it's stylistically different than the style
  of most white preachers. Look for its release in February of 2020 or
  pre-order now"-- Provided by publisher.
Identifiers: LCCN 2019036138 | ISBN 9780802419200 (paperback) | ISBN
  9780802417895 (ebook)
Subjects: LCSH: African American preaching. | Expository preaching.
Classification: LCC BV4221 .S26 2020 | DDC 251.0089/96073--dc23
LC record available at https://lccn.loc.gov/2019036138

Originally delivered by fleets of horse-drawn wagons, the affordable paperbacks from D. L. Moody's publishing house resourced the church and served everyday people. Now, after more than 125 years of publishing and ministry, Moody Publishers' mission remains the same—even if our delivery systems have changed a bit. For more information on other books (and resources) created from a biblical perspective, go to: www.moodypublishers.com or write to:

Moody Publishers
820 N. LaSalle Boulevard
Chicago, IL 60610

1 3 5 7 9 10 8 6 4 2

*Printed in the United States of America*

To Pamela,
My Autumn,
who makes summer of no end for me,
or rather, it always is spring;
you make me preach with joy and laughter.

And to Rev. Terry D. Streeter,
I have no need for some *friendology*
when I have you as my pastor and preaching mentor.

And to Lenny "Mom" Wilson,
You give to scores of children,
and I am thankful to be one of them;
you and your clowns are with me wherever I serve.

—ECR

# CONTENTS

Contributors     9

### PREFACE
The Treasure and Potential of African American Preaching     13
— CHARLIE E. DATES —

### INTRODUCTION
The Joining of the African American Tradition and Exposition     21
— ERIC C. REDMOND —

### PART 1
**Black Preaching and Black Hermeneutic:
A Background for Biblical Exposition**

1. The African American Expositor: Interpretive Location, the
   Plain Sense of Scripture, and Church Life     39
   WINFRED OMAR NEELY

2. A Ladder, a Mediator, and an Ark: The Challenge
   of Old Testament Exposition     55
   ERIC C. REDMOND

3. Contextual Considerations in a Tension-Filled New
   Testament Text     75
   ERNEST GRAY

### PART 2
**Biblical Exposition of the Old Testament**

4. Enough Is Enough: Expository Preaching from an
   Old Testament Pentateuch Book—Deuteronomy 1:1–8     93
   GEORGE PARKS JR.

5. Take Your Mountain: Expository Preaching from an
   Old Testament Historical Book—Joshua 14:6–15     107
   ERIC C. REDMOND

6. Holla If You Hear Me—The Mission of Worship:
   Expository Preaching from an Old Testament Poetical
   Book—Psalm 96                                                   123
   ERIC MASON

7. The Ministry of Vision: Expository Preaching from
   an Old Testament Prophetic Book, Largely Poetical
   —Habakkuk 2:1–4                                                 137
   TERRY D. STREETER

8. His Word Works: Expository Preaching from an Old
   Testament Prophetic Book, Largely Narrative
   —Jonah 3                                                        151
   CHARLIE E. DATES

**PART 3**
**Biblical Exposition of the New Testament**

9. Who Is This Man? Expository Preaching from the Gospels
   and Acts—Mark 5                                                 167
   ROMELL WILLIAMS

10. Have You Got Good Religion? Expository Preaching
    from a New Testament Epistle—James 1:26–27                     181
    PAUL FELIX

11. Waiting for a Wedding: Expository Preaching from the
    Apocalypse—Revelation 21                                       201
    K. EDWARD COPELAND

**CONCLUSION**

12. A Case for a Regular Diet of Preaching through a
    Biblical Book                                                  217
    ERIC C. REDMOND

Acknowledgments                                                    237

# CONTRIBUTORS

**K. Edward Copeland** (JD, University of California; DMin, Trinity Evangelical Divinity School) serves as pastor of New Zion Missionary Baptist Church in Rockford, Illinois. He has been a lecturer for the National Baptist Convention of America, USA Inc., National Baptist Convention of America, Inc., Church of God in Christ, Inc. (Illinois Fifth Jurisdiction West), as well as district associations, conventions, and conferences throughout the nation and across denominational lines. He is a board member of the National Evangelism Team and is a gifted trainer in the areas of evangelism, discipleship, youth ministry, sacred music, and men's ministry. He has a passion for helping ministers and ministries develop to their maximum potential. He is the author of *Riding in the Second Chariot*. Pastor Copeland lives with his beautiful wife, Starla, and their three children, Jibri ("God's hero"), Abeni ("We prayed for her arrival"), and Titus Omari ("Pleasant/New Beginning"), in Rockford.

**Charlie E. Dates** (PhD, Trinity Evangelical Divinity School) is senior pastor of Progressive Baptist Church, Chicago. He serves as an affiliate professor at Trinity Evangelical Divinity School and as an adjunct professor at Moody Bible Institute. Pastor Dates also serves on the Community Advisory Board for the Chicago Fire Department. He is a contributor to the 2014 book *Letters to a Birmingham Jail*. Pastor Dates is married to Kirstie and is the proud father of their children, Charlie Edward II and Claire Elisabeth.

**Paul Felix** (ThD, The Master's Seminary) is senior pastor of Fairview Heights Baptist Church, Inglewood, California, and president of Los Angeles Bible Training School. He is professor emeritus, New Testament, The Master's Seminary, Sun Valley, California.

**Ernest Gray** (PhD student, McMaster Divinity School) is assistant professor of Bible at Moody Bible Institute. He is a graduate of Moody and a graduate of Wheaton College with an MA in Biblical Exegesis. He is a licensed pastor with the Christian and Missionary Alliance. Professor Gray teaches undergraduate students in the areas of hermeneutics, Greek grammar, general epistles, and the Gospel of John. His PhD studies specialize in New Testament Language and Linguistics. He is extremely blessed to have married his wife, Shanya, in 2006, and they are the proud parents of Elias (nine) and Asher (four).

**Eric Mason** (DMin, Gordon Conwell Theological Seminary), aka "Pastor E," is the founder and pastor of Epiphany Fellowship in Philadelphia, Pennsylvania. He and his wife, Yvette, have three sons, Immanuel, Nehemiah, and Ephraim, as well as one living daughter, Amalyah. He is the founder and president of Thriving, an urban resource organization committed to developing leaders for ministry in the urban context. He is the author of four books: *Woke Church*, *Manhood Restored*, *Beat God to the Punch*, and *Unleashed*. Pastor Mason has served as an adjunct professor at the College of Biblical Studies in Houston, Texas, and Biblical Theological Seminary outside of Philadelphia.

**Winfred Omar Neely** (DMin, Trinity Evangelical Divinity School; PhD candidate, University of Aberdeen, Scotland) is professor of Preaching and Pastoral Studies and program head of the Biblical Exposition major at Moody Bible Institute, and senior pastor of Judson Baptist Church, Oak Park, Illinois. He is the author of *How to Overcome Worry*, and a contributor to the *Moody Bible Commentary*, *Moody Handbook of Preaching*, *Heart for the Community*, and *Do Angels Have Wings?*

**George Parks Jr.** (DMin, Union University School of Theology) is pastor of New Hope Baptist Church, with two campuses in North Little Rock and Conway, Arkansas. Pastor Parks's ministry began early under the tutelage of his father, who served as the pastor of

New Pilgrim Baptist Church in Dayton, Ohio. His work is featured in *The African American Pulpit* and *Southwestern Seminary Preaching Source*, and he is the author of *When God's Purpose Finds You: Navigating the Winding Road of Life.* He is married to the former Joy Marie Dailey, and they are the proud parents of George L. III ("Trey"), Genesis, and twins, Gabriel and Grayson.

**Eric C. Redmond** (PhD, Capital Seminary and Graduate School) is associate professor of Bible, Moody Bible Institute, and associate pastor of Preaching, Teaching, and Care at Calvary Memorial Church, Oak Park, Illinois. He formerly served as assistant professor of Bible and Theology, Washington Bible College in Lanham, Maryland, and senior pastor of Reformation Alive Baptist Church, Temple Hills, Maryland. He has contributed to and published several works, including *Where Are All the Brothers? Straight Answers to Men's Questions about the Church.* He and his wife, Pamela, have been very happily married since July 1991, and they have five adult children affectionately known as the "Five Cs": Charis, Chloe, Candace, Calvin, and Codell.

**Terry D. Streeter** (DD, Maple Springs Baptist Bible College and Seminary) is pastor of Mount Pleasant Baptist Church, Washington, DC. He currently serves as dean of the Baptist Education Congress of Washington, DC, and vicinity. He has served as chairman of the Board of Education and Publication for the Progressive National Baptist Convention (PNBC) and the vice-president at large of the Congress of Christian Education for the PNBC. He is the former national dean of the Congress of Christian Education for the PNBC and past moderator of the Mount Bethel Baptist Association, Washington, DC. Pastor Streeter formally served as the evangelism chairman for the Baptist Convention of DC and vicinity. Rev. Streeter is married to the former Sherl Johnson. They have four children and five grandchildren.

**Romell Williams** (Trinity International University and Moody Bible Institute) accepted his call to be the shepherd of Lilydale Progressive Missionary Baptist Church in September 2004 and has committed himself to the spiritual health and growth of the members of Lilydale and the Roseland community. A native of Chicago, Pastor Williams is the firstborn son of Rev. and Mrs. Romell Williams Sr. Rev. Williams represents the third generation of men in his family to preach the Word of God. He accepted his call to the ministry and was licensed at the age of seventeen. He was later ordained at the age of nineteen.

# PREFACE

*The Treasure and Potential
of African American Preaching*

CHARLIE E. DATES

These are interesting times in the development of the African American student of preaching. On one hand, more scholarship on the subject of African American homiletics exists than ever before. On the other, we are witnessing perhaps the greatest identity crisis of the young black homiletician in America. It might appear that the accumulating scholarship would have, by now, defined the role and clarified the function of the sacred tradition of black preaching. The opposite may be the case. Rather than clarifying, some pages within the scope of scholarship may misrepresent the most significant component of black preaching. Today the church and academy are witnessing the rise of the black preacher with a warped view of his heritage and an insufficient appreciation for its foundation. Some, to be sure, as a result of this misrepresentation, are leaving the tradition and heritage of the black church in favor of a kind of gospel gentrification.[1] Others are, with equal indignation, rejecting the authority of the biblical text and the beauty of its complexity in preaching.

This preface seeks to provide a background for the biblical and colorful hermeneutic of black preaching. It proposes that one of the many contributions of black preaching to the overall discipline of homiletics and to the development of the church is its insistence on rightly dividing the Word of Truth and its simultaneous prophetic application of that truth in the absence of societal privilege. One can learn much from a tradition of preaching that emerged from the transatlantic diaspora, is baptized in suffering, is sophisticated in rhetorical harmony, and yet proclaims salvation to the land of its own captivity. This is part of the unique contribution black preaching bequeaths, and it is one that this volume seeks to represent.

Some in the progressive corridors of the academy criticize their brothers and sisters whom, they believe, are held captive to white evangelicalism. Then others in the conservative corridors of the academy remind those in progressive spaces of their captivity to the European Enlightenment. We propose that we need neither

---

1. *Gentrification* is the practice of displacing (typically) lower-income minorities by upper-to-middle-class majority families/individuals in a way that adjusts the property value and in essence causes those original families to lose their homestead.

*Gospel gentrification* is a term I picked up from K. Edward Copeland that exemplifies this same phenomenon in the church and academy. It happens when young black scholars move into white evangelical institutions and are enamored by their supposed theological sophistication and the increased value of their tradition, and, as a result, reject their own. Like a neighborhood being gentrified, the voices of the socioeconomic disinherited becomes replaced with those of the white evangelical giants.

It is happening in record number. More and more black students attend white evangelical schools, sit under white evangelical pastors, and abandon the black tradition altogether. They sit in those pews and consider the ice of white evangelicalism as colder than the ice of their forefathers.

theological slave masters. Ours is a robust, multidimensional, and theologically responsible tradition of preaching. It must be dealt with honestly, studied carefully, and represented truthfully. People of African descent in America were believers long before the transatlantic slave trade.[2] They did not need the flawed slaveholding religion of the Whitefield, Edwards, or the New Divinity to reach the cross of Calvary. One can make the case that Christianity was cradled in North Africa. It was out of *Egypt* that God called His Son (Hos. 11:1; Matt. 2:15). The early church fathers like Augustine of Hippo, Cyril of Alexandria, Origen, Tertullian, and others were brown-skinned men from the land of Africa. Their formulation of Christian doctrine is well attested. What is not so well attested is the ethnic affirmation their work deserves.

For too long, the study of Christian doctrine, its formulation, and the relationships between those doctrines have been hailed as Eurocentric disciplines. That's historically false. Further, the implications of orthodox doctrine upon our preaching should be developed from across the ethnic spectrum. The bounds that those implications provide, which ultimately shapes the application of our preaching, should be printed on a multicolored press. Gospel-centered preaching in America and the coalitions that preserve it can no longer consider such preaching the brainchild of eighteenth- and nineteenth-century White America or sixteenth-century Europe. It is wealthier than that.

At the same time, those who already possess a responsible ethnic affirmation within black Christian preaching can no longer consider themselves superior to those with a high Christology and a high view of Scripture. Historically, within the local black

---

2. See David D. Daniels III, "1619 and the Arrival of African Christianity," Jude 3 Project, August 31, 2019, https://jude3project.org/blog/slavetrade.

church in America, at the grassroots level, several of our most noted voices held both our ethnic value and our Christ in the highest regard with no conflict. Who said we had to choose? Who has bewitched us?

How we handle Scripture both models and trains our churches to read the Bible. If our preaching is irresponsible, we put the church at risk. If the tone of our messages does not match the tenor of the biblical passage, we sell a counterfeit sermon on Sunday morning. If the claims we make about God and His word are false, then our preaching is unreliable, and the people who consume it suffer because of it. If we make it up or believe the lopsided, manufactured, and often fabricated biases of unredeemed scholarship, then we make of the church an impotent army. This volume, by presenting a swath of sermons from some of America's brightest African American preachers, seeks to suggest that we don't have to make it up. We can come to the pulpit with a word from God—a word that the original authors would recognize and that which the God of the Bible ordained. We can preach faithful sermons—messages that are faithful to God and His Word through the homiletical ideas formulated and the Christian actions summoned.

This volume is deliberately about biblical exposition. We confess that exposition is not the sole way to preach. At the same time, we propose that biblical exposition is a most profitable method for Christian preaching. It is not dry, dull, or an empty running commentary. Exposition seeks to expose, to uncover the meaning in the text. It actually believes that there is meaning in the biblical text. It does so through a serious search for the original context, people, and intent of the passage. Yet it does not stop there. Exposition seeks to build a homiletical premise for present-day application. It considers the hopes, failures, dreams, and conditions of people in this present age. It sees in the text a kind of living principle applicable to every age past and every age to come. It finds its fidelity in a trust that the God of the Bible yet honors His Word written long ago. In so doing, the power of this preaching is not the personality of the preacher, though that matters; neither is it in the eloquence of the preacher's voice, or the creativity of the preacher's mind. The power in this preaching is in the God of the text. If the power of God is unleashed by faithful representation of His Word, then those who hear the preacher will experience His power.

At the same time, this is not to say that the Bible is a book to be worshiped; it is not. The Bible is the means by which, as Paul told Timothy, God breathes His life and ideas into humanity (see 2 Tim. 3:16–17). To be faithful in Bible exposition is to worship God, not the book. We hope that by reading these sermons by these pastors you, too, will give this kind of biblical exposition a greater witness. It is preaching in living color.

The literature on preaching with variety abounds. You might wonder what's different about this book. There are texts about preaching with imagination, preaching that keeps Christ at the center, preaching the big idea, varying the genre of preaching, and more. Few texts, however, speak to the color of preaching. That is how to analyze and learn from the cultural nuances of preaching from people of color. This book offers some of the best sermonic examples from a few of the clearest voices within the black Christian preaching community. It is a kind of preaching that considers the nuances of the cultural-historical background of the biblical text from within the uniqueness of the black church tradition and the African American community. I'm not saying that black preaching is monolithic. It is not. There is a discernible thread, however, within black biblical exposition that shares traits from which we can mine principles for preparation and delivery.

For instance, in some practices of black biblical exposition, the sermon title itself is often the sermon's proposition or probing question. The sermon title is important as it is an invitation to explore the main idea of the passage in view of contemporary application. It can be used as an attention-getter, a suspense-builder, and in some cases a proclamation of the sermon's destination. While this is not exclusive to black biblical exposition, the careful selection of a sermon title speaks to the art of preaching. A gift of black preaching to the field of homiletics is its intersection of preaching as science and art. On one hand, preaching has technical elements for exegesis, structure, theological, and doctrinal proclamation. On the other, preaching, like jazz, can move within a structure, an invisible outline, a storytelling that makes the point without necessarily announcing the point. It can invite hearers into the biblical narrative, turn their ears into eyes, and arrest their imagination.

The cultural perspective of the black Christian experience is also an excellent perch from which to view, interpret, and describe the theological narrative of human deliverance. Much of the Bible is written across a cultural landscape of oppression, social unrest, ethnic tensions, and idolatry. The haves oppress the have-nots. The rich lord over the poor. The slaves are servants to masters. The people of God are often complicit in the very injustices of which God's prophets pronounce judgment. Yet God delivers! The redemptive power of God in favor of His rebellious people leaps across the pages of an otherwise hopeless narrative. We both identify with and contrast against the chosen people of God, and the godless society pictured in the text. Here is a privilege within the African American community of homiletics. Ours is a kind of existential identification with the oppressed and socially marginalized. We understand by way of lived experience what cultural disadvantage means. We do not want pity, but our preaching resolutely sounds the bell of authentic confidence in God. In our preaching lives the germ of hope. Historically, we have had nothing else. That, in many ways, is a gift.

Christianity as we've known it—a cultural, political, and populous force—is waning. It is no longer at the center of culture and power in America. It is moving away from the center to the margins of culture. As the Christian landscape in America shifts to the margins, the beauty and power of the African American hermeneutic and homiletic gifts a special witness to the church in America. In these pages, you will find sermons that represent some of that exposition. The sermons here balance the science of preaching with the art of preaching. Some of them are picturesque, vivid, and almost musical. They sing and sting. They are anthropological and theological. In them are insights for preachers and Bible readers who want to be most effective today.

# INTRODUCTION

## The Joining of the African American Tradition and Exposition

ERIC C. REDMOND

### The Question of Favored and Disfavored Preaching

Stop me if you've heard this story before. A mainline church in the African American preaching tradition recognizes the calling of one of its young African American members. The young preacher goes through sort a of grooming process—maybe initially unbeknownst to him. He has grown up in the church and been taught to enjoy its worship music and how to pray at gatherings, often sounding remarkably similar to the pastor. He soon teaches Sunday school and advances to leading Bible studies. Once deemed ready, the young preacher is nominated to be a candidate for licensure and reads Scripture in front of the church on youth Sunday, represents the church in the youth division of denominational meetings, and serves in various roles during revivals and other days within the church's annual cycle of anniversaries. He grows more confident as multiple church members feed him affirmation and as the whispers of the church mothers about the would-be preacher become louder: "That one sho' nuff has been called by God." And just like that, after an initial sermon, a new preacher is birthed into the church.

Wanting the preacher to have some knowledge to go with the burning fire of the call, the church encourages the new preacher to get training at the nearby evangelical Bible college or seminary. All starts well as the young herald advances in theological and biblical studies. However, over the course of the first and maybe even second theological degree, a notable change takes place in the preaching of the future pastor or evangelist. Rather than sounding like someone reared in the shadow of the pulpit in an African American church, the preacher returns from school sounding like a popular evangelical radio and conference speaker.

The people who have sent this young preacher to school no longer identify with the preacher's sermon content. Some say, "That school has made him white," for the preacher's "preaching" comes across to the congregation like "teaching," maybe even like lectures rather than a bad Bible study lesson.[1] There is a clear structure of three or four strong points with theological words reflective of the passage. There are terms from evangelical theology, maybe even references to an ancient creed, historical covenant, or Reformed confession such as "The Heidelberg Catechism says . . ." There might also be quotes from obscure Puritans and some dead persons the preacher calls "divines."

Absent, however, are references to figures in African American history and contemporary African American preachers. There is less story and more abstraction. Most notably, there is little to no

---

1. Zora Neale Hurston's very famous lines in *The Sanctified Church* portray this sentiment as part of African Americans' early history: "The real, singing Negro derides the Negro who adopts the white man's religious ways in the same manner. They say of that type of preacher, 'Why he don't preach at all. He just lectures.' And the way they say the word 'lecture' make it sound like horse-stealing. 'Why, he sound like a white man preaching.' There is great respect for the white man as law-giver, banker, builder, and the like but the folk Negro do not crave his religion at all" (Zora Neale Hurston, *The Sanctified Church* [Cambridge, MA: Da Capo Press, 1998], 106–107).

sense of celebration in the preaching, no "touch your neighbor," no "look at your neighbor and say . . . ," and no "give God a crazy praise!" Over the course of the formal training in Bible and theology, the young herald has been developing a growing disdain for what he believes is "the 'simplistic, unsophisticated' preaching of the black church."[2]

Years later, when another young preacher prepares to go to the same school or one similar, the church warns against acculturation in many ways: "Don't let that school make you white." "Chew the meat, spit out the bones." "Remember where you came from when you get to that school." Or even worse, "That school cannot train people to preach in *our* context."

Why do evangelical ministerial studies sometimes lead to a disdain for preaching within the African American tradition?[3] What could make someone studying *Scripture* reject preaching as a *cultural* artifact? Equally important, why would a pupil of

---

2. The quote derives from a similar vignette, in which Charlie Dates writes, "While studying theology at his small Bible college, he started to run up against the not so subtle jabs aimed at the black church. His professors and his peers wondered why someone so bright would return to the 'simplistic, unsophisticated' preaching of the black church. Far be it from them to name it heresy" ("Don't Give Up on the Black Church," *CT Pastors*, September 2015, https://www.christianitytoday.com/pastors/2015/september-web-exclusive/dont-give-up-on-black-church.html).

3. I recognize this statement is full of conjecture. However, even recently in a conversation with an extremely well-known African American pastor with over twenty-five years of ministry experience, speaking of a nearby evangelical seminary he said to me, "We can't send anyone to that school because they come back useless to do ministry in the Black Church." Similarly, I recently met an African American pastor in an evangelical Doctor of Ministry program who expressed to me, "I like this program because they do not try to make you change your ministry to fit their [cultural] idea of ministry like other [evangelical] schools do." (The context of the conversation concerned the difference between DMin offerings at evangelical schools.) I have had conversations like these too many times in almost three decades of ministry. I suspect many others might have had the same experiences.

theology embrace—often uncritically—the preaching exhibited by his predominantly white, evangelical professors and chapel speakers, the preaching often portrayed as the only form of "biblical" preaching?[4] Are there inherent characteristics that make one ethnic *tradition* of preaching of the Word of God more or less *expositional* than another's? As an African American, is it possible to embrace one's ethnic culture within one's preaching tradition and still give an expositional sermon? Does embracing the African American preaching tradition naturally curtail one's ability to offer expositional preaching? Moreover, is it possible that these questions reveal a misunderstanding about both expository preaching and the African American tradition—a misunderstanding that is like confusing a coat with the coat hanger on which it is draped?

## Clarifying the Meaning of Expository Preaching

It would seem that these questions surrounding African American preaching and the biblical exposition of Scripture concern both the *form* and *content* of preaching. On one hand, some might view exposition to be the opposite of the intoned, poetically embellished sermons with a celebratory closing that often includes "whooping." On the other, some may view the African American contextualized emphasis on justice in the present realm as a "social gospel" that does not derive from the development of the biblical author's ideas

---

4. In agreement with Cleophus J. LaRue, *Rethinking Celebration: From Rhetoric to Praise in African American Preaching* (Louisville: Westminster John Knox Press, 2016), xiii, I recognize "we cannot deepen our understanding of the particulars of black homiletical theory simply by contrasting and comparing ourselves to approaches to preaching espoused by those from another culture." This volume is not an attempt to contrast African American preaching against the preaching of any other ethnic group's homiletical theories or practices.

within a passage of Scripture. I would suggest that neither the form nor content concerns aforementioned necessarily set themselves against biblical exposition when one rightly defines *exposition*.

Consider several recent definitions of expository preaching. Bryan Chapell writes, "The main idea of an expository sermon (the topic), the divisions of that idea (the main points), and the development of those divisions (the subpoints) all come from the truths the text itself contains. No significant portion of the text is ignored. In other words, expositors willingly stay within the boundaries of a text (and its relevant context) and do not leave until they have surveyed its entirety with their listeners."[5]

Similarly, Albert Mohler writes,

> Expository preaching is that mode of Christian preaching that takes as its central purpose the presentation and application of the text of the Bible. All other issues and concerns are subordinated to the central task of presenting the biblical text. As the Word of God, the text of Scripture has the right to establish both the substance and the structure of the sermon. Genuine exposition takes place when the preacher sets forth the meaning and message of the biblical text and makes clear how the Word of God establishes the identity and worldview of the church as the people of God.[6]

Mohler later states, "When it is done rightly and faithfully, authentic expository preaching will be marked by three distinct characteristics: authority, relevance, and centrality."[7]

Each of these definitions makes the main idea of the biblical

---

5. Bryan Chapell, *Christ-Centered Preaching: Redeeming the Expository Sermon*, 2nd ed. (Grand Rapids: Baker Academic, 2005), 131.

6. Albert R. Mohler, *He Is Not Silent: Preaching in a Postmodern World* (Chicago: Moody Publishers, 2008), 65.

7. Ibid., 69.

text the focus of the sermon, whether "expositors willingly stay within *the boundaries of a text*" (Chapell) or "the text of Scripture has *the right to establish both the substance and structure* of the sermon" (Mohler).[8] Exposition is the work of surveying the full text of a set of verses or setting forth the meaning and message of a passage of Scripture. Both of the above definitions are consistent with the classic and oft-quoted definition of biblical preaching by Haddon Robinson: "Expository preaching is the communication of a biblical concept derived from and transmitted through a historical, grammatical and literary study of a passage in its context, which the Holy Spirit first applies to the personality and experience of the preacher then through him to hearers."[9]

The consensus about biblical, expository preaching is that the author's idea in the text is primary. Therefore, the ability to discern and communicate that meaning is important. However, the communication does not require a particular mode of verbal delivery. Expository preaching concerns only the *content* of a message with respect to the words of Scripture and its accurate delivery. Scripture's power for "teaching, rebuking, correcting and training in righteousness" (2 Tim. 3:16) does not demand a certain *style* of expression. The expositor is free to give expression of a text in a manner that brings glory to God by its clarity, faithfulness to the Word of God, and holiness.

Second in sequence, but equally important to the definitions of expository preaching, is the preacher's ability to speak from the Scriptures to contemporary issues for the people of God.

---

8. Since much of expository preaching is about hermeneutics, this volume includes chapters on such in the discussions to come. See chapters 1–3.

9. Haddon Robinson, *Biblical Preaching: The Development and Delivery of Expository Messages*, 2nd. ed. (Grand Rapids: Baker Academic, 2001), 21. Prior to his definition, Robinson identifies expository preaching as the type of preaching that "best carries the force of divine authority," which he equates with "biblical preaching" (20).

The preacher must "correct, rebuke and encourage" hearers from the Word of God (2 Tim. 4:2). Expository preaching concerns "the identity and worldview of the church as the people of God" (Mohler) and "applies . . . to the hearers" (Robinson).

Because expository preaching must speak meaningfully to the preacher's audience, it seems that such preaching—biblical preaching—allows the preacher to utilize a style or mode of exposition that resonates with his audience's contemporary concerns and vernacular. *That is, expository preaching is an invitation for the preacher to explain the central idea of the text to an audience with a means that would be understood by the audience, while exhorting the audience to obey God's Word within that audience's contemporary social and ecclesial contexts.* Expository preaching and African American stylistics are all-star dance partners, not battlefield enemies.

## Theological Emphasis and Style of African American Preaching

Preaching in the African American tradition has certain theological emphases in addition to its distinctive style. Two of these emphases are *justice* and *hope*.

### Justice

African American preaching is part of what Lewis Baldwin calls "that tradition which refuses to separate religious faith and moral considerations from politics, legal matters, and social reformism."[10]

---

10. Lewis V. Baldwin, *The Legacy of Martin Luther King, Jr: The Boundaries of Law, Politics, and Religion* (South Bend, IN: University of Notre Dame Press, 2002), xv, quoted in Rufus Burrow Jr., *Martin Luther King Jr. for Armchair Theologians*, 1st ed. (Louisville: Westminster John Knox Press, 2009), 161. Baldwin is speaking of Martin Luther King Jr.'s identity within the African American preaching tradition.

It readily speaks to issues of race and racism, greed and poverty, and police brutality and the value of human life. It has been a tool for bringing movement toward civil rights in the United States, for speaking out against Apartheid in South Africa, and for promoting the just treatment of both genders and of various sexual orientations without condoning sexual sins and misconduct. Kenyatta Gilbert notes,

> The spoken Word in America's Black pulpits has long been esteemed for its persistent calls for justice, church reform, moral and ethical responsibility, and spiritual redemption. These commitments have been central to the Black church's identity. More importantly, though, these commitments to the spoken Word provide a way to take up the more fundamental matter of how one may, for example, determine what relational continuities exist between the prophets, priests, and sages of Scripture and the basic character of the Black preacher's peculiar speech and communal obligations.[11]

In a similar vein, Robert Harvey suggests, "In the days of past, the clarion call and mission of the black church was two-fold: it served as a beacon of hope for the lost-soul seeking grace and mercy, but it also functioned as an oasis for all issues affecting the community. The black church served as a voice in the wilderness, crying out that equality and justice belonged to all persons, despite race, social status, or lived experience."[12] Included in the church's justice practices was the preacher: "The black minister preached a transformative message of salvation, but also served

---

11. Kenyatta Gilbert, *The Journey and Promise of African American Preaching* (Minneapolis: Fortress Press, 2011), 19.

12. Robert S. Harvey, "Restoring the Social Justice Identity of the Black Church," *Inquiries Journal* 2, no. 2 (2010): 1.

as a community representative and social activist, preaching a message of social change, equality, and unconditional love."[13]

## *Hope*

African Americans' experiences with suffering and injustice profoundly shape the preaching in the African American pulpit. Going to the Bible to find words of hope, comfort, and joy has been part of African American life since the days of slavery:

> In 1792 Andrew Bryan and his brother Sampson were arrested and hauled before the city magistrates of Savannah, Georgia, for holding religious services. With about 50 of their followers they were imprisoned and severely flogged. Andrew told his persecutors "that he rejoiced not only to be whipped, but would freely suffer death for the cause of Jesus Christ. . . ." Slaves suffered willingly because their secret liturgies constituted the heart and source of slave spiritual life, the sacred time when they brought their sufferings to God and experienced the amazing transformation of their sadness into joy. . . . One source that sustained Christian slaves against temptations to despair was the Bible, with its accounts of the mighty deeds of a God who miraculously intervenes in human history to cast down the mighty and to lift up the lowly, a God who saves the oppressed and punishes the oppressor.[14]

Frank Thomas, noted scholar of African American preaching, suggests the ability to transform an individual and nation from despair to hope is a hallmark of African American preaching.[15]

---

13. Ibid.
14. Albert Raboteau, "The Dignity of Faith," *Christian History Magazine* 62 (1999), https://christianhistoryinstitute.org/magazine/article/dignity-of-faith.
15. Frank Thomas, "Black Preaching Changed the Course of this Country," *The Washington Post*, May 9, 2016, https://www.washingtonpost.com/news/acts-of-faith/wp/2016/05/09/black-preaching-changed-the-course-of-this-country-what-creates-that-style/?utm_term=.0add5d24a295.

Sunday to Sunday, preaching in the African American tradition has offered hope to a people who often found little for which to hope in their contemporary surroundings. Even with the unfortunate advent of Prosperity Gospel preaching, *hope* remains a hallmark of African American preaching. This is most evident in the celebration aspect of African American preaching.

Exposition thrives with celebration, and celebration—in its many forms—is best when coupled with the exposition of the Scriptures. Exposition lends its authority to celebration when the celebration arises from the central idea of the sermon, which is the central idea of the text in expository preaching.[16] Celebration, in turn, adorns the greatness of exposition by creating an outlet for the preacher and congregation to share and express the joy of the words from God revealed to them. As Philip Pointer explains,

> Cultivating celebration is vital. Without it, the preacher misrepresents a critical segment of the divine message. Celebration is not anti-intellectual or mere emotionalism. In fact, true gospel celebration is the concert of intellectual understanding, healthy emotions, and the inspiration of the Holy Spirit. God is glorified, the church is strengthened, and unbelievers are shown a clear picture of the spiritual fellowship between a loving God and the redeemed community when these elements come together around the proclaiming and hearing of the gospel. Without celebration we are simply telling news rather than good news.[17]

16. "Expositional preaching is preaching in which the main point of the biblical text being considered becomes the main point of the sermon being preached" (Mark Dever and Greg Gilbert, *Preach: Theology Meets Practice* [Wheaton, IL: Crossway, 2011], 36).

17. Phillip L. Pointer, "The Role of Celebration in Preaching," Preaching Today, https://www.preachingtoday.com/skills/2017/february/role-of-celebration-in-preaching.html.

In order to see that traditional African American preaching—both its style and theological emphases—and exposition complement one another in such a way that both should be thought of positively, lets return to the earlier analogy of the coat and coat hanger. Exposition, because it deals with the biblical text, is the structure that supports biblical preaching. As one explains the words of Scripture within its context, God's voice speaks with authority, because the preacher is communicating what God has said. The preaching is revealing the will of God and calling people to embrace what He wants for us and requires of us. Exposition is a hanger on which any coat of truth may hang.

The African American preaching tradition is just one coat of many that might rest on the hanger of exposition. African American preaching's thrust toward justice and hope are not the exposition of a passage itself. They will derive from the exposition of a cache of passages, but they are not necessarily the coat hanger.

Neither should one think of exposition as the coat. Exposition is not a style. Exposition unveils the message of the text. If one equates exposition with a style, then exposition and African American preaching become antitheses. In the same way, if one thinks of the African American tradition as the substance of preaching, then African American preaching wrongly will suffer epithets that relegate it to something that is sub-exposition. It is not an either/or choice with the tradition of African American preaching and expositional preaching.

## Moving Forward

In the pages to follow, the contributors to *Say It! Celebrating Expository Preaching in the African American Tradition* will show that expositional preaching is not the property of one culture. Neither is it devoid of the ability to hold the attention and change the minds and hearts of congregations through the best use of rhetoric, story, tune, and tone. It is not a white evangelical, Reformed, or academic coat hanger, but simply a coat hanger; it awaits the coat you will drape on it as an African American preacher.

The writers in this work, however, are *not* arguing for the wedding of exposition and African American preaching so that our preaching can be on par with that of a predominantly white evangelical culture. African American preaching stands on its own two feet as some of the greatest preaching in the history of heralding God's Word. It kept and shaped a people through the horrors of antebellum slavery and the chattel dehumanizing of people made in the image of God. It sustained and strengthened a free people through the injustices of Jim Crow and its musclemen of the KKK and lynching. African American preaching was the engine of the civil rights movement—the power that stirred masses to demand equal rights for the descendants of slaves and that gave hope that the American Dream was as much in reach as glory. African American preaching continues to speak truth to power in the post-civil rights—and era for which for many African Americans still is a cauldron of a dream deferred. It does not need to meet par. In the modern world, it establishes par.

Instead, the writers intend to show what is involved in the method of developing expositional preaching, and then show its fitness for you to be able to "*say it!*" I say "show" because many of the chapters contain a full sermon manuscript preceded by an explanation of the process involved in preparing the sermon. The sermons are lightly edited to allow each expositor to speak in the vernaculars, tones, and sanctified theological imaginations used when he preached the sermon in its original setting. *These will be biblical expositions within the African American tradition.*

Part 1 is "Black Preaching and Black Hermeneutics: A Background for Biblical Exposition," which erects scaffolding for preaching by looking at the interpretive theory needed for preaching from the full canon of Scripture. In chapter 1, Winfred Neely explores how the African American experience, honed in the fires of oppression, shaped preachers to be more sensitive to some biblical themes overlooked in the larger evangelical world. In chapter 2, I will attempt to demonstrate that all Old Testament passages are ripe for preaching truth to a contemporary society by considering three representative Old Testament passages. Ernest Gray will do the same for the New Testament, using one representative New Testament passage, in chapter 3.

Part 2 of this volume is "Biblical Exposition of the Old Testament," which includes four sermons derived from four major sections of the Old Testament—the Pentateuch, Historical Books, Poetical Books, and Prophetic Books. In chapter 4, George Parks Jr. provides a sample exposition from the Pentateuch, using Deuteronomy 1. In chapter 5, I exposit Joshua 14:6–15, an Old Testament narrative passage from a book of history. Chapter 6 explores a passage rich in figures of speech, as Eric Mason works through Psalm 96, giving us an example in a poetical passage. In chapter 7, Terry D. Streeter opens the Scriptures in Habakkuk 2 in order to preach through the writing of a prophet largely using poetry as the vehicle of his oracles. In chapter 8, Charlie Dates provides a second examination of prophetic literature by working through Jonah, a prophetic passages that has narrative as its base.

Part 3 considers "Biblical Exposition of the New Testament." Like in Part 2, the contributors consider exposition within macrodivisions of this testament—the Gospels and Acts, the Epistles, and the Apocalypse. In chapter 9, Romell Williams draws from a series of stories in Mark 5 to demonstrate exposition within the

Gospel and Acts, asking, "Who is this Man?" from Mark 5. Paul Felix uses his expositional skills to walk through James 1:26–27 in chapter 10, showing the elements that comprise epistle. In chapter 11, K. Edward Copeland discusses the elements that comprise Apocalyptic literature, and how to interpret this literature within a biblical hermeneutic, looking at Revelation 21.

Finally, in the last section, I argue that preaching through biblical books best allows God's voice to speak organically to a congregation. I demonstrate how exposition through biblical books serves to teach your people how to interpret and to give the lay person a biblical theology.

In the early years of my undergraduate teaching, I was invited to give an evangelistic sermon at an outdoor event for a traditional African American church in Washington, DC. The person introducing me had read my biography, emphasizing my education and academic ministry, even though I had seven or eight years of church ministry under my belt by this time. Before anyone had time to be unimpressed with my background, a person a few feet from the outdoor preaching platform shouted from the audience, "Yes, but can he preach?" The question was not a concern about my ability to give an exposition of the Scriptures. Instead, all present understood that the hope was that the education that trained me to do *exposition* would not get in the way of bringing a message that would move the crowd as a sermon falling within the African American *tradition*. Thankfully, my training did not get in the way; neither is it inherent that training in exposition works against the tradition. The coat and hanger go together like flesh on bone.

Every time the church gathers for corporate worship, one should find strong preaching and exciting celebration! The young preacher of an evangelical educational experience should not dismiss the black church tradition in fear of coming in conflict with exposition of the biblical text. Expositional preaching explains the text, teaching people the oracles of God. Expositional preaching can communicate messages of justice and hope.

Exposition can reveal a God who is a battle ax, a bridge over troubled waters, a way-maker, a fence, a doctor in the sick room, a lawyer in the courtroom, a rock in a weary land, a shelter in a time of storm, a balm in Gilead, and one who can hit a straight lick with a crooked stick! The God of the expositor can "pick you up and turn you around, place your feet on solid ground."[18] Expositional preaching also hangs Jesus high and stretches Him wide on the cross, gets Him up early on Sunday morning, and get us to King Jesus soon and very soon! *Exposition and the tradition are best when they hang together.*

---

18. Edwin Hawkins, "If You Come to Him" (Indianapolis, IN: Tyscot Records, 1997).

# PART 1

# Black Preaching and Black Hermeneutic: A Background for Biblical Exposition

# THE AFRICAN AMERICAN EXPOSITOR

*Interpretive Location, the Plain Sense*
*of Scripture, and Church Life*

## WINFRED OMAR NEELY

### All Of Us Have an Interpretive Location

> Every generation has a story.
> Every ethnic group has a story.
> Every culture has a story.
> Every family has a story.
> Every person has a story.

Human beings are storied creatures, and having a story is an essential element of what it means to be human, to be a person created in God's image.

Embedded in all of our stories is the impact of key people (parents, relatives, close friends, mentors, influencers, leaders, abusers, oppressors, and so on) and key events (praying with your mother or father, affirming moments from a friend, physical abuse, rape, terrorist attacks, and more), key people and key events that have shaped us and molded us for good or for ill.

Embedded in all of our stories are scripts—that is, patterns of behavior with expectations about roles and conduct in various life situations. We learned, acquired, and internalized these patterns of behavior and scripts because we are members of a family, a culture, an ethnic group, or citizens of political entities such as the United States, France, Senegal, or Ghana. In discussing how we acquire scripts, Linda Kay Jones writes:

> We learn, or grow into, identifying patterns in human behavior. We learn certain scripts just by being human. Other scripts we learn as members of our culture. (And of course this culture idea can be extended into any little subculture group that a person may belong to, in which the person learns the scripts of that subculture.)[1]

And beyond the horizon of our individual and familial narratives and scripts, the mental life, generational scripts, and perspectives of entire generations have been shaped by key events and key people. The World War 2 generation of Europe and the United States;[2] the Jewish holocaust survivors; the post-September 11, 2001, generation; and Generation Z, shaped and molded by the American great recession of 2008, serve as examples of this phenomenon.

As a result of our stories, and all of the experiences in life that make up the warp and woof of our stories, each one of us has what Jeannine Brown calls "an interpretive location."[3] She employs the

---

1. Linda Kay Jones, *Theme in English Expository Discourse* (Lake Bluff, IL: Jupiter Press, 1977), 117.

2. During World War II, African American soldiers were treated with respect and dignity by Europeans. With their mental horizons expanded and altered as a result of their experience in the war, these veterans returned to the United States determined to no longer accept second-class citizenship in their own country. This alteration of their mental horizon was one the catalytic factors in the civil rights movement of the 50s and 60s.

3. Jeannine K. Brown, *Scripture as Communication: Introducing Biblical Hermeneutics* (Ada, MI: Baker Academic, 2007), 121–22.

spatial metaphor of "location" as the cultural, social, and experiential place from which we construe the world and vantage point from which we interpret life, people, and texts, including the Bible. This metaphorical "location" is our entire perspective and the limit of our cognitive horizon from which we view the world. All of us bring all we are to the interpretive table of life and texts. In short, every one of has an interpretive location. We are not neutral. Thus, one of the first steps in our study of Scripture is to acknowledge that we have a social location. This step is important because our interpretive locations and cultural scripts shape how we interpret and misinterpret life. Moreover, and more fundamentally, our interpretive faculty itself is fallen and as a result we come to texts with warped horizons with the propensity to twist reality into our own image. Therefore, a chastened hermeneutic of humility is always in order when we interpret life, culture, texts, and the Bible.[4] Kevin Vanhoozer reminds us:

> In an age that views interpretation in terms of violence and coercion . . . charity is needed more than ever. There is something in the text that is not of the reader's own making. The . . . reader must not violate but venerate this "other." For readers come not only to knowledge but also to self-knowledge when they allow the text to have its say.[5]

The recognition that we all have an interpretive location prepares us to be better readers of Scripture and should move us to study Scripture with an attitude of humility.

---

4. Kevin J. Vanhoozer, *Is There a Meaning in This Text* (Grand Rapids: Zondervan, 1998), 32, declares, "Life together is largely *interpretation; good hermeneutics* makes *good neighbors.* The Golden Rule, for hermeneutics and ethics alike, is to treat significant others—texts, persons, God—with love and respect" (emphasis added).

5. Ibid.

While all of us have a defective interpretive faculty, our interpretive location, which is the product of culture and experience, may hinder us from noticing or paying closer attention to some aspects of Scripture or may give us blind spots. For example, in her book *Scripture as Communication*, Jeannine K. Brown, writes,

> I am Caucasian and from a middle-class white-collar economic and educational sector of society. As a result, I have enjoyed the social advantages and power of being in what has been the majority culture in this country. . . . One way my social location has affected how I read the Bible is the rather large blind spot I have inherited and preserved related to wealth. This blind spot has caused me to neglect the pointed biblical emphasis on God's care for and championing of the poor and the frequent warnings about the dangers of wealth.[6]

It is important to note that Brown's blind spot in her own words was inherited and was a product of her upbringing. Interpretive faculty and interpretive location are not the same, but they are related.

Indeed, our interpretive location may make us more sensitive than others to elements of biblical truth that others may miss or may not appreciate as much as we do. For example, Brown also notes:

> My family of origin, my gender, my familial roles as wife and mother, being a musician, my earlier career in a social service field, as well as the events I have experienced in my life thus far—all these and more influence my interpretive vantage point. Becoming a parent for me had profound theological impact, as I was swept up in a love for my children that gave me a new appreciation for God's love.[7]

---

6. Brown, *Scripture as Communication*, 122.
7. Ibid.

Since all Christ followers have an interpretive location, and since all of us may have blind spots or experiences that may make us more sensitive to aspects of scriptural truth that others with different experiences may miss, we need one another as we grow in our knowledge of God based on His Word. In this chapter, therefore, our consideration of the hermeneutics of the African American expositor of Scripture is not a discussion limited to the African American experience, but a discussion that is beneficial to the entire body of Christ.

## The Interpretive Location of the African American Expositor

The experience of African Americans in the United States shapes the African American biblical expositor. The historical memories of slavery, Jim Crow, lynching, the desperate fight for the recognition of inherent human dignity, the open casket of Emmett Till, the assassinations of Medgar Evers (37 years old), Rev. Dr. Martin Luther King Jr. (39 years old), and Malcom X (39 years old) are but a few of the events that mark the African American experience. Other significant events also shape our consciousness, including ongoing violence and poverty in some African American communities, the growth of the prison industrial complex and mass incarceration, and the election of Barack Obama as the first African American president of the United States.[8] These experiences create a profound sense that we, as a people, have "come this far by faith . . . leaning on the LORD."[9] But that sense recognizes that precious lives

---

8. A person must not agree with all of President Obama's political policies and views in order to appreciate the historic significance of his election.

9. Albert A. Goodson, "We've Come This Far by Faith" (Manna Music, Inc., 1965, 1993).

have been lost to injustices in the process, and that the blood of African American men and women and children has been spilt through the fruits of this nation's racism, discrimination, and prejudices, and the ongoing legacy of its white supremacy movements.

Today, the African American expositor stands on the shoulders of African American followers of Christ who had the courage before God to assert their worth and value as image bearers and Christ followers. All of these experiences are part of the interpretive location of the African American expositor in a general sense.

The ironic miracle of providence is also a part of the African American expositor's interpretive location. In this sense, the African American preacher embodies one of the ironic miracles of providence and represents church life in the African American community as an ecclesiastical miracle:

> Within the black community, the church has played an absolutely constitutive role. One of the ironies of history is that African slaves in America were indoctrinated in the religion of their master, yet discovered the true, liberating meaning of the gospel over against its cultural distortions. This happened in large part through the so-called invisible institution, the underground church that gathered secretly to sing, pray, shout, preach, and read. Here there occurred what might be described as a clearing of freedom within the harsh domain of oppression, a clearing in which slaves were transformed in human beings, seemingly silent docile masses into a singing, resistant, hopeful people. Throughout much of black history, individuals found their true dignity and identity precisely and only in the black church— in that space of freedom cleared on Sunday morning and Wednesday evening, or whenever the community gathered. . . . The black church is a spiritual, eschatological, transformative event which has proved to be constitutive of the very survival of a people.[10]

When African Americans, with colossal oppression and hardship seared into their social locations, encountered the biblical text, a redemptive revolution of hope, courage, and strength occurred. This is one of the great ironies of God's gracious providence in the African American experience in the United States. Not even slavery, Jim Crow, racial prejudice and discrimination, and systemic racism embedded in the very laws of this land, and not even the abuse of Scripture to support these injustices, were able to stop the penetrating power of the gospel in the African American community. This miracle is also a part of the informed African American's interpretive location.

Yet also standing in these spaces was and is the African American preacher, declaring freedom in the midst of a harsh world of oppression! Since the preacher by and large shared the social location of this people, the preacher was used by God as His instrument of blessing to this community. Under God, black preachers were at the helm of this powerful, spiritual, eschatological, and transformative event of black church life that has resulted in the survival of an entire people in the United States.

Under God, the preacher's task was to keep hope alive in the hearts of many black men and women followers of Christ who lived life at the razor-sharp edge of hopeless circumstances. This was a part of the preacher's preaching ministry and a vital part of the pastoral care of the African American church congregation. *The preaching moment is pivotal in this endeavor.* Think of the boldness of the expositor who has wrestled with God and emerged with the courage to say to these beautiful and oppressed people, "Let not your hearts be troubled!"

---

10. Peter C. Hodgson and Robert C. Williams, "The Church," in *Christian Theology*, eds. Peter C. Hodgson and Robert H. King (Philadelphia: Fortress Press, 1985), 267.

## Convictions about the Bible

African American expositors like Rev. James T. Meeks,[11] Tony Evans, Crawford Loritts, H.B. Charles, Byran Loritts, and Charlie Dates approach their pulpit work with certain convictions about the Bible. The Bible is the divinely inspired word of God, and as such the Scriptures are without error in all that they assert and claim in their autographs. The Bible is the supreme and ultimate standard and final authority for faith and practice. As an expositor of the word of God, like any other preacher committed to expository preaching, the African American expositor has made the decision to bend his thought toward Scripture instead of bending Scripture toward his thought. Thus, the African American expositor reads and interprets Scripture in its plain, normal, and overt grammatical sense.

## Sensitivity to the Plain Sense of Scripture

It is at the juncture of the plain, literal, surface structure sense of Scripture and the social location of the African American expositor where redemptive life-change occurs first in the preacher, and then through the preacher to the African American congregation. The social location of the African American expositor made the preacher more sensitive and receptive than preachers of different social locations to some texts of Scripture.

The African American interaction with early chapters of the book of Exodus show powerfully the response of the African

---

11. In his opening message at the 2018 Founder's Week conference, Pastor Meeks affirmed the divine inspiration and the inerrancy of Scripture. He is also a trustee of Moody Bible Institute. Every year each Trustee signs our doctrinal statement, which includes the Chicago Statement on Inerrancy.

American social location in the interpretive process. These passages portray God's children, Israel, in the throes of slavery and state-sponsored genocide—one of the darkest periods in Israel's history. God's people were powerless to free themselves and oppressed. Early African American expositors resonated with the slavery and genocide of these texts, for it spoke representatively to their experience in the United States. These texts became a major source of strength and a basis for instilling the will to survive injustice in the hearts of African American congregants. The following text serves as an example:

> Now it came about in the course of those many days that the king of Egypt died. And the sons of Israel sighed because of the bondage, and they cried out; and their *cry* for help because of their bondage *rose* up to God. So God *heard* their groaning; and God remembered His covenant with Abraham, Isaac, and Jacob. God saw the sons of Israel, and God took notice of them. (Ex. 2:23–25 NASB, emphasis added)

For the African American expositor and listener, each verb in the verse is brim full and running over with hope—God heard, God remembered, God saw, and God took notice of them. African Americans, both enslaved and free, took great courage and hope in the fact that God hears the groans of *slaves* and that their cries for help reach God Himself. Preaching on texts that narrate the courage in the midwives in the face on an oppressive regime, the preacher was able to say that God cared for slaves and knows their situation as no one else could. Deep spirituality and understanding of the character of God developed out of this insight. As we sing,

Nobody knows the trouble I've been through,
Nobody knows my sorrow.
Nobody knows the trouble I've seen,
Glory Hallelujah![12]

These three lines of profound sorrow were accented by a daring line of hope; the same daring lines of hope accent African American biblical preaching.

Yet, this was not easy. The preacher wrestled with God and with His Word in view of the harsh and cruel experiences that the people endured daily. The age-old question of the oppressed, "Where is God. . . . Where is God now?"[13] dotted the landscape of many African American preachers. While many slaves did not experience deliverance, they learned in the crucible that, literally, all they had was Jesus, and they took great courage and strength in the fact that God heard their cry!

It seems strange that under this kind of preaching, African American followers of Christ who lived through slavery came out with their souls and sense of dignity intact. Several years ago, the late Gardner Taylor told me that when he was a little boy in Louisiana, he knew men and women in the church where he fellowshipped who had come out of slavery, but they were not broken. They wanted to do something with their lives. They knew that the Lord had heard their cry. Taylor said to me that these men and women marked his life. The pain of the African American expositor's social location resulted in them being sensitive to the biblical idea that the God of glory, the King of Kings, and the Lord of Lords hears the cries of people in bondage. This truth became to many

---

12. See "Nobody Knows the Trouble I've Had," in *Slave Songs of the United States*, William Francis Allen, Lucy McKim Garrison, and Charles Pickard Ware, eds. (New York: A. Simpson & Co., 1867).

13. Elie Wiesel, *Night* (New York: Bantam Books, 1982), 61–62.

African American preachers and congregants "a sword, a shield, a hammer, it became their life motivation, their good hope, and their confident expectation."[14]

## *Church Life*

The pastoral care of the preacher for the African American congregation demanded that the preacher help them see themselves from God's point of view. These preachers generally embraced a robust biblical view of people in their preaching and in the churches they pastored; they placed great emphasis on the biblical view of human worth, value, and dignity.

Moses's authorship of the first five books of the Bible has huge significance in these communities. The Mosaic authorship of the Pentateuch means that these books were addressed to a people recently liberated from slavery. In deliberation with Himself, God said,

> "Let Us make man in Our image, according to Our likeness; and let them rule over the fish of the sea and over the birds of the sky and over the cattle and over all the earth, and over every creeping thing that creeps on the earth." God created man in His own image, in the image of God He created him; male and female he created them. (Gen. 1:26–27 NASB)

The African American expositor understood that a people fresh from slavery needed to understand who they are. They are image bearers; slavery was the result of the fall and not God's creative intent. Their preaching evinced pronounced sensitivity to the idea that all people—and yes, black people—bear the image of God. They did not attempt to give people dignity, but preached

---

14. A. W. Tozer, *The Knowledge of the Holy* (New York: HarperCollins, 1961), 80.

the Word to help them understand and embrace the redemptive and existentially healing facts that they possess inherent dignity due the fact they bear the image of God. This pastoral effort was so vital because of the way a hostile white world defined them. They heard messages everywhere that they were cursed, that they were inferior, that they did not matter, that they did not have a soul, that they were not human. Disrespected and mistreated in the world, these men and women of dignity were affirmed and celebrated in the preaching in their local churches. The biblically informed assertions "I am a man," "I am a woman," or "I am somebody" are bold affirmations in an oppressive world. Under the guidance of faithful biblical preaching, these men and women learned to allow God and God alone to define them.

The interpretive location of African American expositors makes them incredibly sensitive and alert to the plain teaching of Scripture about the value of children. In a world that was dangerous for children—and some parts of our country are still dangerous for black, brown, and white children—these passages leap out with force to the African American expositor. "Jesus loves the children"[15] resonates deeply with these preachers as they read,

> Then people brought little children to Jesus for him to place his hands on them and pray for them. But the disciples rebuked them.
> Jesus said, "Let the little children come to me, and do not hinder them, for the kingdom of heaven belongs to such as these." When he had placed his hands on them, he went on from there. (Matt. 19:13–15)

From this passage, the preacher inculcates a love for the

---

15. C. H. Woolston, "Jesus Loves the Little Children" (n.d.).

children. Making a connection to his congregation was possible immediately because the African American church was (and remains) a place where children are nurtured, protected, and treasured. It was from the interpretive location that the African American preacher proclaimed—with uncommon depth—the biblical mandate to love and care for children (Matt. 19:13–15).

Historically, African American expositors have understood that people are not pure spirits, but embodied beings. As such, the implications of the gospel expressed themselves in ministries that addressed the needs of the whole person—spiritual, social, and physical. As a result of this kind of biblical exposition, churches developed banks, credit unions, insurance companies, and colleges. They embraced the larger implications of the gospel for all of life.

By and large, the African American expositor does not approach Scripture in a surgical and detached way, but from the vantage point of the African American interpretive location, the preacher engages the imagination as a vital part of the interpretive process. In the preaching moment, the African American expositor will sometimes appeal to the imagination of the congregation, inviting them to engage their imagination as the message is preached. Thus, the use of the imagination in the study and the appeal to the listener's imagination in the pulpit play key roles in African American exegesis and exposition. As the late E. K. Bailey observed,

> If I were planning to preach about John when he was on the isle of Patmos, I might take this approach. In my sanctified imagination, I would walk with John on the isle of Patmos and let him show me the ins and outs of that isle. Then I would begin to walk my people through various experiences . . . they have in their own lives. . . . Because I have "transported" myself there through the text, the people go there with me as I explain John's words. They

see the text through me because I have stepped into that text and internalized it. I come to the pulpit and in an incarnational way open up my experience so that they are enveloped in the scene and identified with the message it brings. . . . It is the genius of exposition and application conveyed at times either by story-telling or direct exposition, and the utilization of imagination and creativity, that makes the text intimate and personal.[16]

But something must be said about what happens when the African American congregation meets the plain sense of Scripture through the faithful exposition of an African American preacher. Woven into the social location of both preacher and congregation is call and response. The cultural expression of a verbal call from a speaker, and the verbal response from listener finds its roots in centuries old traditions of African culture. It is beyond the scope of this chapter to discuss the African origins of call and response in African American church life, but suffice it to say that preaching in the African American tradition is not a verbal monologue. The African American preacher does not stand alone in the preach-ing moment. Audience participation and verbal and nonverbal response is a vital and unique part of the preaching experience in African American church life. As Henry Mitchell notes,

Black preaching has been shaped by interaction with the listen-ers. If the Black preaching tradition is unique at all, then that uniqueness depends significantly upon the uniqueness of the Black congregation, which talks back to the preacher as a normal part of the pattern of worship.[17]

16. E. K. Bailey and Warren W. Wiersbe, *Preaching in Black and White* (Grand Rapids: Zondervan, 2003), 45.
17. Henry H. Mitchell, *Black Preaching: The Recovery of a Powerful Art* (Nashville: Abingdon Press, 1990), 100.

In response to the preached Word, a person or persons in the audience will respond with expressions like "well," "preach," "go head on and preach," "say that," "my Lord," "yes sir!," "Amen," "Praise the Lord," "Sho'nough!," and many other spontaneous audible responses.[18] The response sometimes is nonverbal, swaying the body, raising the hands, tears, foot patting, shouting, tears, standing up and nodding the head in affirmation of the message, and clapping.[19] As Mitchell observes, "Whatever the form, the communication is real."[20]

Sometimes the preacher asks the audience for support,[21] such as "Can I get a witness?", "Are you all with me or am I by myself?" Sometimes the organist and the pianist will respond to the call of the preached word.

In African American church life, audience participation generally is expected. Christian worshipers in the African American expression of church life and worship feel authorized to express themselves freely in response to the preached Word. These kinds of informed responses are used of God to provide meaningful participation in the preaching moment. These moments are times of blessing for both congregation and preacher. Indeed, as Mitchell has pointed out,

> Few preachers on any race can deny that their powers are enhanced in the spiritual dialogue that takes place with the authentic Black congregation. Most preachers of any culture would gladly welcome such stimulation and support every Sunday, if it were to be offered by their congregation.[22]

---

18. Ibid., 101.
19. Ibid.
20. Ibid.
21. Ibid.
22. Ibid., 100.

To this day, in response to the preached word, men and women and boys and girls leave these sacred spaces of corporate worship ready to face another day in the name of Jesus. Both preacher and congregation have experienced God in corporate worship, and have affirmed this experience through words and gestures, tears and hope as they have encountered the God of the plain sense of Scripture. Indeed, it was the teaching of the plain sense of Scripture that the Lord used to put survival strength into a whole people and preserve them to this day. To God be glory!

CHAPTER 2

# A LADDER, A MEDIATOR, AND AN ARK

*The Challenge of Old Testament Exposition*

## ERIC C. REDMOND

## INTRODUCTION

Preaching the expansive literature in the 39 books of the Old Testament can seem like a daunting task. The storyline covers at least two thousand years from Abraham to the last word in Malachi. Many of the books themselves are long, including 50 chapters in Genesis, 52 in Jeremiah, 66 in Isaiah, and 150 in the Psalms. The books of two volumes, which each really would do well to be held together as one-volume works, are just as long with 55 chapters in the Samuels, 47 in the Kings, and 55 in the Chronicles. These 475 chapters alone could provide 8 years and 2 months' worth of weekly preaching, and that is if one does not subdivide any of the chapters, but preaches each chapter as one unit, including Psalm 119! Preachers have their hands full when attempting to tackle preaching the Old Testament.

In addition to the sheer length of the Old Testament, many theological, moral, and ethical dilemmas pose quite the interpretive and application challenges to heralds and hearers alike. The preacher must address the Old Testament saints' polygamy, plagues as judgments, murders and rapes, years of enslavements and oppressions for God's people (as those innocent in Exodus, and as those guilty in Judges and the exilic period), and great suffering with theodicy as the only answer. One cannot avoid these issues while working through the Old Testament, especially since they contribute to how God is bringing a people to Himself in redemptive history.

Moreover, preaching the Old Testament requires the expositor to understand how multiple genres work to communicate their meaning. This includes law, narrative, poetry, prophecy, and the subgenres within each of these domains.[1] Then there remains for the preacher to preach the gospel from the Old Testament, unveiling the New Testament from the Old Testament and revealing the Old Testament from the New Testament, as Augustine expressed:

> To the Old Testament belongs more fear
> just as to the New Testament more delight;
> nevertheless in the Old Testament the New lies hid,
> and in the New Testament the Old is exposed.[2]

---

1. There are many nuances within these genres, including Old Testament parable, wisdom, and covenant lawsuit. For more on interpreting the various genres of the Old Testament, see Gordon Fee and Douglas Stuart, *How to Read the Bible for All Its Worth*, 4th ed. (Grand Rapids: Zondervan, 2014); Sidney Greidanus, *The Modern Preacher and the Ancient Text: Interpreting and Preaching Biblical Literature* (Grand Rapids: Eerdmans, 1989); Walter C. Kaiser Jr., *Preaching and Teaching from the Old Testament* (Grand Rapids: Baker, 2003); Tremper Longman III, *How to Read the Psalms* (Downers Grove, IL: IVP, 1988); Leland Ryken, *Words of Delight: A Literary Introduction to the Bible* (Grand Rapids: Baker, 1993); Christopher J. H. Wright, *How to Preach and Teach the Old Testament for All Its Worth* (Grand Rapids: Zondervan, 2016).

2. Quoted in David L. Baker, *Two Testaments, One Bible: The Theological Relationship Between the Old and New Testaments* (Downers Grove, IL: IVP, 2010) 38.

Or again, as Augustine wrote more simply, "Wherefore, in the Old Testament there is a veiling of the New, and in the New Testament there is a revealing of the Old."[3]

## The Problem of Genre

Interpreting the Old Testament books according to their various genres is extremely important. One does not read Genesis 1–2 and apply them the same way one reads Psalms 8 and 136, even though all four places address the creation of the cosmos. They were not intended to be read or interpreted the same way.

My task in this chapter is to argue that passages within the various genres of the Old Testament are equally readily accessible and relevant for one to preach. That is, one is able to interpret these passages for preaching without feeling that some passages are inaccessible or irrelevant for a contemporary audience. In order to present this argument, I will briefly explore three Old Testament passages: Genesis 28, Exodus 2, and Psalm 24, showing their foreshadowing of the gospel and relevance to modern believers.

## Genesis 28:10–22

How do we discern the point of Genesis 28:10–22, and its significance to us as believers in Christ? The story is unusual, relaying Jacob's dream of a huge stairway in the middle of the episode.

---

3. Augustine, *On the Catechising of the Uninstructed*, 4:8, http://www.newadvent .org/fathers/1303.htm. This last quote comes in popular form as, "In the Old the New is concealed; in the New the Old is revealed" (Lat. *Novum Testamentum in Vetere latet, Vetus Testamentum in Novo patet* [Augustine, Questions on the Heptateuch, Hyde Park, NY: New City Press of Focolare / Augustinian Heritage Institute, 2016 2,73: PL 34, 623].)

Let us consider the items in the text as presented to the readers/
audience.

First, *Jacob's dream about the ladder occupies the most*
*space, so it must be the most important part of the passage*
(28:11–17). Everything else in the passage revolves around
the dream. Jacob's actions in 28:18–22 come as a result of
the dream, for without the dream, one would expect him
to get up the next morning and keep going toward Haran
(see 28:10). Also, with respect to the dream, it connects
Jacob's story to the Abrahamic covenant narrative (see Gen. 15:12–
21; 17:15–16, 19, 21; 26:1–4; 27:26–29; 28:1–5). Consider in particular
the words of 28:13–15:

> There above it stood the LORD, and he said: "I am the LORD, the
> God of your father Abraham and the God of Isaac. I will give
> you and your descendants the land on which you are lying. Your
> descendants will be like the dust of the earth, and you will spread
> out to the west and to the east, to the north and to the south.
> All peoples on earth will be blessed through you and your off-
> spring. I am with you and will watch over you wherever you go,
> and I will bring you back to this land. I will not leave you until I
> have done what I have promised you."

"The God of your father Abraham" connects Jacob to the
one who was faithful to Abraham during his full sojourn from age
seventy-five until his death. The blessings and promises of Abraham are passed to Isaac and then to Jacob. The promises of land
inheritance, descendants like dust of the earth, and the mediation
of blessing to the whole world harken to the original words of
promise and the words of God's covenant with Abraham (Gen.
12:3; 15:5, 13, 18–21). The connection to Abraham is significant because God is accomplishing His plan to re-establish His rule over

and through man on the earth through the line of Abraham. The dream reiterates the promises, again emphasizing the universal scope of the promise—the entire earth will be blessed through Jacob's offspring.

Second, *the dream itself is unique*. "The sun had set" (28:11) takes the reader back to Gen. 15:17, cluing the reader to expect that something like the covenant might take place. It would seem unnecessary to tell us that Jacob used a stone for a pillow unless that stone is a key to what happens later. This is evident to the reader because the Genesis writer does not inform us of anything about Jacob's pajamas or nightly grooming rituals!

The stairway reaching from earth to heaven is reminiscent of the Tower of Babel (11:4), so the reader should expect God to show up in judgment if this stairway is not pleasing to Him. However, one immediately finds "the angels of *God*" and "the Lord" associated with this stairway. These particular angels are coming up and down from God to the earth. These are significance details of the dream. Seemingly, the angels are coming from God, as He is above the stairway.

Moreover, Jacob himself recognizes that the dream means he is in the very presence of God, and that he is unaware that he is in God's presence until God reveals Himself through the staircase (28:16–17). *So it seems that the staircase between heaven and earth has something to do with revealing God to someone who does not know he is in God's presence*. Having recognized God's presence, Jacob renames the place "Bethel," which means "house of God." Thus, the dream is associated with God's house. The dream also introduces the reader to the stairway being "the gate of heaven."

Third, *the dream changes Jacob, just a little*. He is the trickster who has beaten his brother out of his birthright and blessings for the oldest son. Jacob is on the way to find a wife, with little concern about God before now. Yet, when this episode ends, Jacob has five responses:

1. Jacob recognizes God's presence, even though he has not recognized it before the dream (28:16), and this provokes fear and worship in Jacob;[4]
2. the stone that he has made his pillow becomes a pillar of anointing (28:18);
3. Jacob realizes his need for God in his life going forward, saying, "If God will be with me and will watch over me on this journey" (28:20);
4. he dedicates himself to God, but conditionally (28:21); and
5. he promises to pay God a tithe of his blessings (28:22), so the dream transforms Jacob's life.

Fourth, *the New Testament helps us better understand the dream by telling us that Jesus is the staircase.* Jesus says to Nathaniel and disciples, "You will see 'heaven open, and the angels of God ascending and descending on' the Son of Man" (John 1:51).[5]

---

4. Nahum M. Sarna, *Genesis: The JPS Torah Commentary* (Philadelphia: Jewish Publication Society, 1989), 199, comments on Gen. 28:16, "This reaction of amazement is unprecedented in the patriarchal stories. Neither Abraham nor Isaac exhibit any surprise at their initial experience of God's sudden self-revelation. Jacob's exceptional emotional response requires explanation. Undoubtedly it lies, at least partially, in his realization of the baseness of his behavior toward his father and brother. He must have been beset with feelings of complete and deserved abandonment by God and man. Having fallen prey to guilt and solitary despair, he is surprised that God is still concerned for him. At the same time, 'the place' he has stumbled upon possesses no intrinsic value for Jacob. It is merely a convenient spot where he may lodge for the night."

So, here's what we have so far: *Jacob's dream of the ladder of God transforms him on his journey from one living without God to one dedicated to God.* This idea ties Genesis 28:10–22 together as one unit.

Having knowledge that Jesus is the ladder, we can insert this knowledge into our statement regarding the identity of the ladder. Also, theologically speaking, "dreams" in Scripture fall under the systematics category of "special revelation." In the progress of revelation through redemptive history, the Lord continues to speak through His Word—also special revelation—even after He ceases to speak via dreams. Therefore, I would suggest the meaning of the story could be restated this way: *Jacob's word from God about Jesus being the staircase of God—the One who is between earth and heaven mediating the Abrahamic blessing of God—transforms Jacob's life.*

Since we are preaching to new covenant believers in the church, and not to a second generation of post-Exodus Israelites, and since we find Jacob to be uninterested in the Lord in the beginning of the story, in my statement of meaning we will replace "Jacob" with modern *unbelievers* and add what we know about the "house" and "gate" to our statement of meaning: *God's word about Jesus being the mediator between heaven and*

---

5. The quotation marks in the NIV suggest that the NIV understands John 1:51 to be quoting Gen. 28:12. Commenting on this verse, D. A. Carson, *The Gospel according to John* (Grand Rapids: Wm. B. Eerdmans Publishing, 1991), 163–64, writes, "The explicit parallel is drawn between Jacob and Jesus: the angels ascend and descend on the Son of Man, as they ascended and descended on Jacob (for clearly that is how John understands Gn. 28:12). . . . Even the old Bethel, the old 'house of God,' has been superseded. It is no longer *there*, at Bethel, that God reveals himself, but in Jesus . . . just as later on Jesus renders obsolete such holy places as the temple (2:19–22) and the sacred mountains of the Samaritans (4:20–24)."

*earth—between man and God—can transform a life in the church (that is, house of God) from unbelief to that which recognizes that Jesus is the gate to heaven.* In short, Genesis 28:10–22 calls us to introduce Jesus as the only mediator in our proclamation of the gospel—and this to unbelievers in our midst, in our pews, in our relationships. This is the story of *the stairway to the house of God.* The interpretation of all narratives works in a very similar manner.

## Exodus 2:11–24

Exodus 24:11–24 contains a story perhaps as well-known as Jacob's dream. Moses, still living in the house of Pharaoh, king of Egypt, sees an Egyptian "beating a Hebrew, *one of his own brethren*" (11 NASB, emphasis added). Apparently identifying with the Hebrews and finding injustice with the beating, Moses takes it upon himself to intervene. In truth, *Moses is attempting to rescue his Hebrew brother.* This is the direction the story takes from the outset of the story.

The next day, still identifying with his brothers, and seeing two Hebrews fighting, he asks, "Why are you hitting your fellow Hebrew?" For Moses, it is one thing for the Egyptians to beat the Hebrews; it is equally wrong in Moses's sight for two Hebrews to fight one another, for they are "fellow Hebrew[s]" (v. 13). This now is a second attempt by Moses to intervene into the life of a Hebrew brother.

The response of the Hebrew brother is telling. First, he interprets Moses's intervention as an attempt to become "ruler and judge over" the Hebrews. Second, the Hebrew rejects Moses's intervention, for he fears that Moses is not there with good motives, but with evil motives—that Moses intends to kill one of the brothers even as he did the Egyptian. Third, although Moses did not see anyone around at the time of the killing, the murder is known. As a result, Pharaoh goes after Moses to kill him.

Thus far, one might summarize the movements in the story in this manner: *Moses attempts to be a rescuer of his Hebrew brethren by killing the Egyptian oppressor. His attempt is in conflict with the Hebrews's and king of Egypt's rejection of Moses becoming king because of his attempt to resolve a conflict between two of his Hebrew brethren in the same manner he attempted to be a rescuer of his Hebrew brethren.* Moses's attempt to intervene on behalf of his brethren seems to be part of both of the first two scenes.

The episode changes scenes as Moses flees Pharaoh and lands in Midian. Yet Moses has an intervening itch at this point in this life. So, the reader can almost anticipate what might happen with Moses watching the scene unfold between the seven daughters of the priest of Midian and shepherds who try to drive away the daughters' father's flock (2:17). Moses comes to their rescue—he intervenes between the daughters and the shepherds so that the daughters can water their father's flock. Upon intervening, Moses then waters the flock for the daughters; he intervenes for them and then serves them.

The remainder of the story shows the responses to Moses's intervention on behalf of the daughters. The story comes to completion as Moses flees to Midian, where *he thwarts men trying to take advantage of the daughters of the priest of Midian and rescues them*, and is welcomed into the home of the Midianite priest and given his daughter's hand in marriage and a son through her, while Israel continues to groan out to the Lord.

The author constructs the story so that the unifying idea is quite evident. First, Moses attempts to be a rescuer of his Hebrew brethren. Next, Moses attempts to resolve a conflict between two of his Hebrew brethren. Lastly, Moses thwarts men trying to take advantage of the daughters of the priest of Midian and rescues them. The ideas are unified by *Moses stepping between people* in all three situations. That is, Moses *attempts to be a mediator* in all three situations. The passage is about *Moses's attempted role as mediator.*

The rest of the elements of the passage concern the welcoming of Moses into the home of the Midianite priest, the priest giving Moses his daughter's hand in marriage, and the marriage yielding a son, while Israel continues to groan out to the Lord. The passage also indicates that *God looks upon the groaning of the Israelites after the death of the king in Moses's absence.* This literary element did not fit into other patterns within the passage. However, one must account for this idea in order to ascertain the message of the entire passage. I propose the following idea for the passage:

> *Moses's attempted role as mediator is condemned by his own Israelite brethren and the king of Egypt because of their disdain for his rule, but gains him an invitation into the home of the Midianites and a Midianite son of acceptance, during the period in which Moses is away and Israel groans under a new king and is heard by the Lord.*

In the above statement, by saying, "Moses's attempted role as mediator," I recognize that in each of the scenes of this passage, Moses steps between two parties. In two of the scenes he delivers one party (the Hebrew brother or the daughters) from another (the Egyptian or the men at the well). In the other, he tries to bring about peace between two Israelite brothers, but is unsuccessful. Hence, we speak of his *attempted* role.

The phrase, "Condemned by his own Israelite brethren . . . because of their disdain for his rule," recognizes that both the Israelite brother questioning Moses and the king of Egypt are threatened by Moses. The Israelite fears that Moses is asserting his power, and the king has concern for Moses rising to become king.

In saying, "gains him an invitation into the home of the Midianites," we are reflecting that the Midianite daughters receive Moses into their home after he rescues them. Through them, Moses has a son—one whose name speaks to Moses's sojourn on earth in a land foreign to him. It is *during the period in which Moses is away*—after Israel has rejected the one attempting to be their mediator, that Israel, still in slavery, groans to the Lord for help. The Lord hears and remains faithful on the basis of the covenant.

## Reviewing Genesis 28 and Exodus 2

The Jacob dream episode and the Moses mediation episode both are narrative genre. They both operate on the basis of *plot*. Plot is *the intentional sequencing of the movement of a story from beginning to middle to end as the story revolves around a goal, a conflict or series of conflicts, and the resolution thereof.* All narratives in both the Old and New Testaments operate on the basis of a plot. Discerning the plot movement will help reveal the meaning of a narrative passage.[6]

For example, the original goal of the Jacob dream sequence is for Jacob to go to Haran (Gen. 28:10). If the story is not interrupted by the dream, Jacob would have awakened in the morning in verse 12 and kept heading toward Haran rather than resuming the journey in 29:1.

---

6. For more on this theory of interpreting narrative, see Eric C. Redmond, "The Very Right of God: The Meaning of Luke 13:1-9, and Criticism(s) of John Piper's View of the Role of God in Tragedy: A Narrative Analysis," in *The Theory and Practice of Biblical Hermeneutics: Essays in Honor of Elliott E. Johnson*, eds. Forrest Weiland and H. Wayne House (Silverton, OR: Lampion, 2015).

This goal comes into conflict with the dream of the staircase (28:11–15). The dream of the staircase is a hurdle to the immediate fulfillment of the literary goal—of Jacob going to and reaching Haran. Also, as the dream takes up the most space in the narrative, one knows that it is directing the reader toward the subject of the passage, for the subject always is the most talked about idea in a passage.

In response to this conflict, Jacob (fearfully) realizes he is in the place of God, makes an altar from his pillow, vows to make the Lord his God conditionally, and promises a tenth of his accumulated wealth to God (28:16–22). These acts resolve the plot so that the episode comes to a close. All narratives work generally in a like manner.

Again, in the example of the Moses mediation narrative, the goal is for Moses to attempt to be a rescuer of his Hebrew brethren secretly (Ex. 2:11–12). This goal comes into conflict with the Hebrew brother's and Pharaoh's rejection of Moses becoming a ruler over them. They both see Moses seeking to rule because of his attempt to resolve a conflict between two of his Hebrew brethren in the same manner in which he attempted to be a rescuer of his Hebrew brethren by killing the Egyptian (Ex. 2:13–15).

The resolution of this plot has many parts; it must include all that is not yet accounted for in the development of our plot. In this passage, in order to address the conflict to the goal, Moses flees to Midian, where he thwarts men trying to take advantage of the daughters of the priest of Midian and rescues them. Then the daughters and the priest of Midian welcome him into their home. Afterward, the priest grants Moses his daughter's hand in marriage, and Moses gains a son through her. Finally, during the absence of Moses, Israel continues to groan out to the Lord and the Lord hears them.

As noted above in the brief analysis of Exodus 2:10–25, Moses's attempt to be a mediator occurs in the first three scenes of the passage. In our plot analysis, *Moses's attempt to be a mediator* occurs in the goal of the story and its resolution. The writer talks about this more than anything else in the passage, so it points to the main idea of the passage.

You might now be wondering to yourself, *Can such an expressly theological and historical passage preach to a modern congregation of the baptized?* Consider, however, that a person determines to *receive* or *reject* Jesus as mediator on the basis of one's view of one's personal need for help or intervention, even as the characters in Exodus 2:10–25 *receive* or *reject* Moses as mediator on the basis of one's view of one's personal need for help or intervention. Very practically, therefore, you could preach a sermon titled "Where Is Moses When We Need Him?" Here are some suggested points in your outline:

1. Moses took responsibility to help when one of his own was in trouble (2:11–12)
2. Moses was rejected as helper because his helping implied that he would rule (2:13–15)
3. Moses was received when the daughters saw he helped them and their families (2:16–21)
4. Moses will return to Israel when the Lord responds to their cries (2:22–25)

It will not be difficult to leap from here to Christ crucified for us if one substitutes "Jesus" (as Mediator) in the place of "Moses" in the outline, and works through the appropriate biblical theology of divine mediation within the progression of revelation through the remainder of the biblical canon. Stephen does this for us in

Acts 7:23-29 and 7:35, and concludes that the typology of this story points toward Jesus (Acts 7:51–53).

## Psalm 24

Psalm 24 is an Enthronement Psalm. Traditionally, Enthronement Psalms might be one of two categories: those that celebrate the Lord's kingship over creation (29, 48, 93, 95, 96, 97, 148), or those that celebrate the Lord's kingship in giving deliverance to Israel and judgment to the nations (46, 47, 98, 99).[7] Psalm 24 seems to contain elements of both types of enthronement.

In terms of the form of the psalm, Enthronement Psalms tend to display a *hymn of celebration*, *an entrance liturgy*, and an *enthronement liturgy*. Psalm 24 has four lines of a *hymn of celebration* (1-2); an *entrance liturgy* of two questions (3), response (4-5), and an affirmation (6); and an *enthronement liturgy* consisting of a declaration (7), a question (in response to the declaration, 8a), a response (8b–9), a repeated question (10a–b), and further response (10c-d).

Within the hymn of celebration (1-2), *David recognizes God as sovereign over the creation based upon His role in the creation.*[8] Stating that the entire earth—its contents and inhabitants—are the Lord's, the psalmist depicts the Lord to have providential ownership over the elemental and inhabited world. The psalmist establishes a logical basis for this truth: The Lord is owner by virtue of being the Creator of these entities (v. 2).[9] One first discerns the

---

7. Willem VanGemeren, "Psalms," in *The Expositor's Bible Commentary, Volume 5,* ed. Frank E. Gaebelein (Grand Rapids: Zondervan, 1991), 32.

8. I assume Davidic authorship because the superscription to the psalm identifies him as the author.

Lord's ownership over the entire creation by analyzing the a b a[1] b[1] pattern in the two sets of parallel lines in 24:1:[10]

| a) The earth is the Lord's<br>b) and everything in it | Physical earth and its elements (e.g., "everything") |
|---|---|
| a[1]) the world<br>b[2]) and all who live in it | Political earth and its inhabitants (e.g., "all who live in") |

"For he founded it on the seas and established it on the waters" (v. 2) alludes to Scripture's initial revelation about the Spirit of God to support David's argument: "Now the earth was formless and empty, darkness was over the surface of the deep, and the Spirit of God was hovering over the waters" (Gen. 1:2), and "And God said, 'Let there be a vault between the waters to separate water from

---

9. "The emphatic particle *ki* (for) sets the conditions of ownership" (James L. Crenshaw, *The Psalms: An Introduction* [Grand Rapids: Eerdmans, 2001], 157).

10. *Parallelism*, the key genre element for understanding the working of poetry, is the sharpening or focusing of meaning in two or more lines of poetry. Following Robert Lowth's *Lectures on Sacred Poetry of the Hebrews* (1753), an older definition of parallelism said that it is the *repetition* of meaning in two or more lines of poetry. The idea was that the second (and third, and fourth lines, etc...) only repeated the first line in different terms. However, work by Kugel, Berlin, Alter, and Garrett have advanced the discussion. See Robert Alter, *The Art of Biblical Poetry* (New York: Basic Books, 1985); Adele Berlin, *The Dynamics of Biblical Poetry*, rev. and expnd. (Grand Rapids: Wm. B. Eerdmans, 1985); Duane A. Garrett, *Proverbs, Ecclesiastes, Song of Songs* (Nashville: Holman Reference, 1993); James Kugel, *The Idea of Biblical Poetry* (New Haven, CT: Yale University Press, 1981).

water.' So God made the vault and separated the water under the vault from the water above it. And it was so" (Gen. 1:6–7).

In the entrance liturgy (Ps. 24:3–6), *the psalmist defines who is qualified to go to Jerusalem to worship in the Lord's presence.* The full picture of the qualified worshiper—one able to ascend to Jerusalem into the place of worship—emerges from the parallelism as one who is righteous in works (v. 4a), motives and thoughts (v. 4a), worship (v. 4b), and the acts of the mouth toward another member of the Israelite community (v. 4c). This worshiper would be a keeper of the fifth, tenth, second, and ninth commandments. Thus, this is the depiction of one faithful to the entire Sinai covenant. This one is righteous in all aspects of living—a faithful member of the covenant community.

The psalm holds out the promise of reward for individual righteousness of these members, including "blessing" and "vindication" (or *justice*). This generation of worshipers show themselves to be a remnant of seekers of the Lord. Only they are those who are going to Jerusalem to worship as those qualified to worship in the experience of which David speaks (v. 3).

This generation-remnant is associated with "Jacob."[11] They are sojourning up ("ascend") to Zion ("the mountain of the LORD") to worship the Lord ("stand," "seek him," "seek your face") in His place of worship ("in his holy place").

Turning to the enthronement liturgy (vv. 7–10), the psalmist calls for the gatekeepers to recognize the Lord Almighty as the King of glory. In a parallel pattern, David calls to some unidentified "gates" and "doors" to "lift" their "heads." Since the temple had not been constructed in David's day, the "gates" must be those that

---

11. VanGemeren similarly identifies this group as "the elect in Jacob" and "the true descendants of Jacob" ("Psalms," 220, 223).

allowed entrance to the city of Jerusalem. The writer personifies the gates as one who is sagging his/her head (for an unspecified reason).[12] However, the gates now must take a posture of rejoicing—which, for the doors of the city, would be to open wide—because the King is approaching.[13] The picture of these doors as everlasting seems to transcend those of the city of Jerusalem, a city built within the time-bound world of the Jebusites and Israelite descendants.

The exhortation to open the gates is associated with the coming of "the King of glory." The designation "King of glory," mentioned five times in verses 7–10, limits the description of the approaching figure to God Himself, as no created being could claim this title rightly. Yet it is apparent that there are some—whether the gatekeepers or others in the city—who do not recognize the identity of this King: "Who is this King of Glory?"[14] It is then that the entire sojourning remnant responds with the identification of the King: "The LORD strong and mighty, the LORD mighty in battle" (v. 8).

Seemingly, the pilgrims intend to *enthrone* this King of glory because He is returning victoriously from battle. Nowhere does the history of David or any of the kings of Israel record such an experience. This indicates that David is speaking *prophetically*.

---

12. Leland Ryken, James C. Wilhoit, and Tremper Longman III, eds., "Gates," in *The Dictionary of Biblical Imagery* (Downers Grove, IL: InterVarsity, 1998), 322.

13. Ryken, Wilhoit, and Longman, "Gestures," in *The Dictionary of Biblical Imagery*, 327. The term "afn" denotes "to stand proudly" (Victor Hamilton, "afn," *New International Dictionary of Old Testament Theology and Exegesis* [Grand Rapids: Zondervan, 1997], 3:163).

14. Raymond Dillard and Tremper Longman see gatekeepers in view (Tremper Longman III and Raymond Dillard, *An Introduction to the Old Testament*, 2nd ed. [Grand Rapids: Zondervan, 1994], 244). One should note such that a reference to Ps. 24:3 does not appear in the index of the work.

Matthew 21:1–11 makes a connection between the events of Jesus's triumphal entry into Jerusalem and Psalm 24:7–9. Some of those with Jesus as He *ascends* and enters Jerusalem (Matthew 20:17–18; 21:1, 10) *recognize* Him as Israel's King (20:21; 21:1, 5). Matthew 21 depicts a *first advent fulfillment* only, because Christ is headed into battle at the cross. The far referent of which David prophesies is of another day awaiting a *second advent fulfillment*.[15] In that day, the Lord will enter Jerusalem as the victorious King of glory to be enthroned, and worshiped as King over all creation.

*David's recognition of the Lord as King guides his understanding of the worship of the King.* David recognizes the Lord as King over the earth, in the lives of those who seek Him, and as the victorious warrior on our behalf. Straight is the line from Psalm 24 to the gospel story of Christ "ruling and defending us, and in restraining and conquering all his and our enemies."[16]

## CONCLUSION

Exposition of the Old Testament is challenging, but it is doable. Recognition of the facets of each passage's genre is important to its correct interpretation. The remainder of the Old Testament canon is just as exciting, accessible, and applicable as Genesis 28,

15. Peter Craigie, without giving specific reference to a Matthean fulfillment, sees a "certain logic" to the Christian use of Psalm 24 "[to affirm] the victory achieved by Jesus Christ in death and resurrection and anticipat[ion] of the ultimate and triumphant Advent of the King," (Peter C. Craigie, *Word Biblical Commentary: Psalms 1-50*, [Dallas: Word, 1983], 215). See also, J. Barton Payne, *Theology of the Older Testament* (Dallas: Word, 1965), 519. Payne refrained from classifying this psalm as "distinctly Messianic" because verses 7–10 "were fulfilled in David (the N.T. truth may be similar, but there exists no real identity)."
16. "The Westminster Shorter Catechism in Modern English with Scripture Proofs and Comments," WSC website, Question 26, https://matt2819.com/wsc/.

Exodus 2, and Psalm 24. The task we have as preachers is to pray for the Spirit's illumination of the meaning of the passage, recognize the genre clues of a passage, and carefully discern the biblical theology trajectory of the themes in the passage that reveal themselves as one continues through the Old Testament into the New. Preaching the ideas that God has deposited in each passage becomes doable when we start with the original meaning of the Old Testament passages themselves and from there travel their lines to the cross of Christ.

# CHAPTER 3

# CONTEXTUAL CONSIDERATIONS IN A TENSION-FILLED NEW TESTAMENT TEXT

## ERNEST GRAY

## INTRODUCTION

A fellow pastor once shared a personal story with me about his reticence to carry out a matter of church discipline. The situation was common; many other churches had experienced it. Yet he was wary of the outcome. A young unmarried couple revealed to him that the young lady was pregnant. The pastor knew he needed to tell the church elders about the situation, but he was anxious that the couple would feel rejected and part ways with the church.

The couple already had one foot out of the door. His fear was not unfounded.

In a bygone era, a simple solution would be to inform the couple to get married and salvage the circumstance. One bad choice of premarital sex need not jeopardize the young couple's faith. Many young adults had faced similar circumstances and needed to navigate similar circumstances. Today, however, the remedy of marriage is prescribed less often and for reasons that relate to the maturity of the couple.

Unplanned, unexpected pregnancies are not relegated to one demographic. Further, every conception of life in the womb is yet another example of God's goodness and promise of future blessing to humanity. While human anxiety around the welcoming of a newborn baby is a reality many couples face, God has used the complexity of an unplanned pregnancy, complete with all of its accompanying fears and anxiety-inducing circumstances, to bring salvation into the world. In this way, Scripture does not sanitize the human experience. The account of the Messiah's birth reminds readers that some of the complexity so common within normal everyday life is also present within the miraculous birth of the Lord Jesus Christ. Indeed, the birth of Christ is no mere pregnancy, and perhaps one could argue that comparisons to any other pregnancy are fool-hardy. Yet this pregnancy and birth were not the result of sin. The tension-filled account, like the one recounted above, demands that expositors approach the Scriptures that record the unexpected pregnancy of Mary with a modicum of caution toward the potential peril that her pregnancy could create.

## Cultural Competence

Indeed, a distinction must be made due to the immaculate conception of Mary the mother of the Lord Jesus. Yet to understand the impact that an unexpected out-of-wedlock pregnancy would have had in the Matthean narrative, let us look at the Jewish literature on the subject.[1] Within the Mishna, the first major written collection of oral Jewish traditions, the tenuous situation would

---

1. For a helpful introduction to the concept of culturally competent interpretation see Brian Blount, *Cultural Interpretation: Reorienting New Testament Criticism* (Minneapolis: Augsburg Fortress, 1995).

place the young lady in serious legal peril and could potentially lead to a divorce. The following is from tractate Sotah 1.1:

> A. He who expresses jealousy to his wife [concerning her relations with another man (Num. 5:14)].
> B. R. Eliezer says, "He expresses jealousy before two witnesses, and he imposes on her the requirement of drinking the bitter water on the testimony of a single witness or even on his own evidence."[2]

And in Sotah 1.5:

> A. [Now] if she said, "I am unclean," she gives a quittance for her marriage contract [which is not paid over to her], and goes forth [with a writ of divorce].
> B. And if she said, "I am clean," they bring her up to the eastern gate which is at the entrance to Nicanor's Gate.
> C. There it is that they force accused wives to drink the bitter water,
> D. and they purify women after childbirth and purify lepers.
> E. And a priest grabs her clothes—if they tear, they tear, and if they are ripped up, they are ripped up—until he bears her breast.
> F. And he tears her hair apart [Num. 5:18].

---

2. Jacob Neusner, *The Mishnah: A New Translation* (New Haven, CT: Yale University Press, 1988); quoted in Darryl L. Bock and Gregory J. Herrick, eds. *Jesus in Context* (Grand Rapids: Baker, 2005), 49.

> G. R. Judah says, "If she had pretty breasts, he did
> not let them show. And if she had pretty hair, he
> did not pull it apart."[3]

The items contained in this exposition relate to the appearance of infidelity. In Matthew 1:18–23, while not stated explicitly, the reader is informed that the pregnancy is due to the Holy Spirit. When one encounters the account of Scripture, clear distinctions between common unplanned pregnancies and the clearly unique circumstances surrounding the conception of Christ must be made. And while both would induce considerable tension and fear, Mary's pregnancy was not due to sin. Hence, when considering the impact that the retelling of this story would have on the original audience, one could infer from the scriptural warrant as well as the cultural expectation, that Mary would be in great peril. Unwed women were thought to have participated in some type of sin that would have resulted in this pregnancy. Indeed, if Joseph divorced her, he would undoubtedly have ground to proceed, and thus would have exposed Mary to peril. Yet as the text unfolds, we find a foil in the narrative in the manner that Joseph reacts to the news. His actions demonstrate a keen awareness of the uniqueness of this situation, and yet he chooses to be used by God to accomplish this task.

## Tools for Our Task

As practitioners who specialize in the public proclamation of the Word, it is necessary for us to be familiar with the tools of our trade. To hold the reality of our human frailty in tension with the

---

3. Neusner, *The Mishnah*, 448; quoted in Bock and Herrick, *Jesus in Context*, 49–51.

informative insights that are gained from Scripture, certain tools aid us to communicate the core truth of the Scripture. Among the tools that remain indispensable are any and all texts that relate to the discipline of hermeneutics.

Integral to biblical exposition are the insights that each interpreter brings to the text. Therefore, prior to utilizing an actual text, keen observation serves as one of the best ways to ascertain the meaning of a biblical text. Items to be scrutinized that I shall list are not exhaustive but represent some of the personal work that each interpreter must do prior to reaching for an interpretation manual from the shelf.

First, when approaching a biblical text, note items in the grammar and syntax—not just verbals and imperatives—but the subtle nuances, like meaning within entire clauses. This will help you to see the meaning emerge at a detailed level.

Second, note well the sentential structure. How does the author state the information? In the case of this Matthean account, the author uses a great deal of conjunctions to tie the meaning together.

Third, look for bulky terms. Words that are not clear upon an initial reading should be marked as candidates for a word study.

Fourth, try to make as many observations within its immediate co-text to see how it fits within the discourse. If written down and organized, this will help the interpreter to generate fresh ideas prior to utilizing the more ubiquitous books for the hermeneutical task. Not only does this aid our ability to thoroughly ascertain the meaning of the text in its home, it allows us to gain a level of proficiency in using them from week to week.

As noted above, one of the most important steps within the process of interpretation remains a keen awareness and sensitivity to the contextual elements. Once understood, contextual elements can be powerful items to implement into the sermon.

## Message of the Text

Matthew 1:18–22 is a distinct unit nestled between the end of the genealogy and the beginning of the Magi narrative. As the story unfolds, one sees that the meaning pertains to the birth account of Jesus Christ.

### Observations

Immediately, the narrative shares with the readers a very common human reality—an unwed pregnancy that puts a couple in crisis. After the revelation of the drama that normally follows such a situation, we are informed that the husband, Joseph, of the young mother, Mary, does not pursue litigation or any other normal means of separation (1:19).

Verse 20 reveals the support and correction for the decision by the betrothed husband. The author indicates that an angelic emissary informs him that the child is not the product of human relations. This is arguably the most important shift within the entire episode. This information, disseminated at a moment when the betrothed husband was weighing his options, introduces a need for a course adjustment.

As readers, we are told that the child born to Mary is to be called "Jesus"[4] (1:21). The child's name bears salvific overtures and intimates that He will save His people from their sin. The narrative

---

4. The English "Jesus" translates the Greek Ἰησοῦς (*Iesous*). In the LXX, Ἰησοῦς translates the Hebrew יְהוֹשֻׁעַ and יֵשׁוּעַ, both rendered in the English as "Joshua" (William Arndt, Frederick W. Danker, et al., *A Greek-English Lexicon of the New Testament and Other Early Christian Literature* [Chicago: University of Chicago Press, 2000], 471–72). As David Howard observes, "Joshua's name means 'Yahweh saves' or 'Yahweh delivers'" (David M. Howard Jr., *Joshua* [Nashville: B&H Publishers, 1998], 27).

concludes with a recapitulation of the prophecy intimated from the book of Isaiah.

## Explanation

The narrator explicitly states that this episode concerns the events surrounding the birth of Jesus Christ. To say that they are betrothed and that the event happened before Mary and Joseph came together is to say that Mary is an unwed mother. In fact, she would have been a pregnant teenager. This is the sort of thing that could have brought about Mary's stoning (see Deut. 22:23–24). Certainly, it would have brought ridicule and shame upon Joseph.

Just when it would seem appropriate to march Mary down the center aisle of the synagogue to have her stand before the congregation and confess her sins, the writer indicates that Joseph, acting righteously according to the law of God, decides to get out of the betrothal legally, but quietly—without fanfare, calling attention to Mary, or shaming her. This is a strong resolution on his part, but one also that is full of mercy.

It is while he is making his righteous ponderings—in accordance with the Law and full of mercy—that an angel of the Lord speaks to Joseph in a dream. The angel will speak to Joseph's fear(s) associated with marrying the expecting young girl, informing him of several things about the child.

First, *the pregnancy is from the Holy Spirit* (v. 20), confirming for Joseph what the reader already knows via the narrator. There has not been an affair or a rape but a miracle. The triune God is the one responsible for this pregnancy.

Second, *the child will be male*, in fulfillment of the promised male offspring of Eve who would do battle with evil and evil's seed and be triumphant (v. 21; see also Gen. 3:15). By acting righteously and with mercy, Joseph will become a witness to God's fulfillment of His plan for the ages.

Third, *the child is the Savior of Israel* (v. 21). The name Jesus means "Yahweh saves," or maybe better, "Yahweh is salvation." This son, Jesus, will be the one to rescue His people. However, the rescue effort does not begin externally with the dispossession of Roman occupation and oppression. Instead, it begins internally— inside of each member of Israel—addressing their personal and corporate sins.

Sin is the great barrier between humans and God; missing the standard of God's righteousness and its subsequent judgment is the thing from which people most need to be saved. Without that salvation, all other salvations are temporary, not being able to sustain because of sin's propensity toward selfishness and abuse of power; not being able to prepare the one saved from human oppression from the everlasting judgment of God. Jesus will over- come that great barrier of sin and rescue people unto God.

Fourth, Mary's *pregnancy fulfills Scripture* (vv. 22–23). Mary is the long-awaited virgin of Isaiah's prophecy (Isa. 7:14). What God had promised to do in the eighth century BC, He now brings to completion in one pregnant girl with one child by the Holy Spirit. This child, named Jesus, will be the child who is "Immanuel." In this child, God Himself will come and be present with His people.

These four pieces of revelation are enough for the righteous Joseph to continue to act with mercy, as he obeys the command of God through the angel. Joseph is obedient to what the angel has spoken from the mouth of God. Joseph, therefore, is willing to forego the legal separation and to embrace the coming shame because the Lord has spoken.

The writer is careful to note that the conception originates in a virgin who is still a virgin at the time of birth: he says the couple is betrothed and the pregnancy happened before they came to-gether. The child is from the Holy Spirit. Mary is identified as a virgin, and Joseph did not know her sexually until after the birth of the child. This righteous man overcame this challenging situation by acting with mercy, being sensitive to God speaking, and being obedient to the voice of God.

## *Relevance*

In tandem with the observations and explanation of the text, and prior to the assembly of the final message, the preacher should think about the contemporary relevance of the passage. As noted above, the coterminous elements of this text for a modern-day audience reside in its ability to speak to the real-world dilemma of unexpected pregnancy. However, the author leverages the occurrence through reassurance to the parties involved—reassurance that overcomes the common elements of fear and shame. This is an example of how the biblical text is able to speak clearly to the human condition in every instance.

## Model for the Message

Among the various models that can be utilized in arranging the meaning for the interpretive task, a model following Haddon Robinson would serve best to tell the story.[5] The method is apt for it is one of the best ways to aid the reader to hear the text and comprehend the flow of the plot. I have adapted the method to involve proposing a Title, Exegetical Idea, Homiletical Idea, Sermon Aim, Probing Question, Exposition, and Close:

---

5. See Haddon W. Robinson, *Biblical Preaching: The Development and Delivery of Expository Message*, 3rd ed. (Grand Rapids: Baker, 2014).

## Title

Hope Born in the Midst of Chaos

## Exegetical Idea

Joseph's godly response to the revelation of Mary's unwed pregnancy allows for Scriptures to be fulfilled concerning the birth of Christ without bringing shame on Mary or himself.

## Homiletical Idea

*Jesus, Messiah, comes to earth in the midst of chaos.*

## Sermon Aim

To invite my audience to contemplate the hope and help Jesus' birth brings to people struggling with dilemmas as great as teen pregnancies.

## Probing Question

What does the account of Jesus' birth indicate about God?

## Exposition

What does it mean for God to be with us? As I have pondered lately, I have come to the conclusion that God never meant for us to be marooned. We were not meant to be placed upon the earth to fend for ourselves. Indeed, we were disobedient in the garden. However, God had an ultimate plan for us. In creating a way to bridge the gap and rescue us from our isolated condition, He sent His Son, the Lord Jesus. This is the most significant graceful act that He has ever done. We are no longer isolated from Him and thus are ever at His side; God had pledged to be with us.

The passage underscores that the glorious predictions of the messianic promises did not disclose the lowly circumstances of the Savior's coming. In fact, we are told that God used the frailty of the human institution of marriage to highlight the complexity of this passage.

In this passage, we see some wonderful dynamics between a young couple. Young couples are faced with many challenging situations. I am convinced that there are significant stresses upon young couples and that this passage does not seek to ignore them. In fact, verse 19 illustrates that due to the seemingly twisted circumstances of fate, Joseph was uncertain of his wife's fidelity. Nothing could bring a more devastating blow to a young engaged couple than to discover that one lover is being unfaithful.

God, however, is not forestalled by Joseph's fears, nor are His promises abrogated by this situation. No, it all is a part of His divine plan. God is utterly committed to humans being recipients of His goodness—and in this case, that goodness came in the form of complex human affairs. I am even more convinced that this is what really matters in life. Not so much that all people have all of their ducks in a row—because that does not render them impervious to disaster—but that each person relates to God and recognizes their utter dependence upon Him. I am pleased to see that God would utilize the lowly circumstances of Christ's birth, "while they were there, the time came for the baby to be born, and she gave birth to her first-born, a son. She wrapped him in cloths and placed him in a manger, because there was no guest room available for them" (Luke 2:7).

What does this passage say to people in our time?

This text is God's glaring reminder that in spite of the condition of our world, God cared enough to subject His own Son to violence to save His people. We live in a violent world. We live in a world plagued by problems, but God has allowed us to be made alive in His Son, the Lord Jesus Christ. By leading the plan to restore humanity to its original design, God sent Jesus at the right time, by the Spirit of God, to a lowly town called Bethlehem to make sure that we would know that His timing is impeccable. God attends to humanity's need by sending His Son.

With the advent of Christ, we are secure in God's universal plan. We are the beneficiaries of God's manifold grace and we can access His resources at our disposal. This newfound relationship will never diminish:

"It's not good," God said. "What's not good?" you ask. "His being alone. Look at him, wandering around the Garden of Eden by himself."

*God* saw that it wasn't good for man to be alone. So He caused a deep sleep to fall on Adam and He gave him someone he could relate to, someone who would share the glories of earth with him: a *woman*—Eve. And later He would give Adam and Eve more humans to whom they could relate: *children*. It's clear, right from the beginning of the Bible, that God created us to be attached to others. But maintaining and nurturing those attachments, those relationships—that's tricky due to the chaos that sin has caused in the world.

I am convinced that God in His grace has allowed us to become attached to Christ in a most healthy sort of way, despite the chaos of this world. Jesus is the help God sends to redeem us from the chaos of this world so we can enjoy the goodness God intended for us in this creation and in the world to come. We see this as Jesus enters the story of Joseph and Mary.

The first way we see the help of Jesus is by noting that chaos must concede to the sovereignty of God (Matt. 1:18–19). God's plans are not minimized by human frailty. This is the hope God brings to our lives. When we are faced with formidable odds and the outcome looks bleak, we can rest in the arms of God when all hope seems lost.

I don't know about you, but had I not known the rest of the

story, I would have been sorely mistaken about the way this Messiah enters the world. In reading all the glorious expectations about the arrival of our Messiah, we might be led to believe that His arrival would be met with fanfare and confetti. However, He comes to the earth in the midst of *chaos—family* chaos, family drama, deep family dysfunction. From glorious predictions and grand expectations to *lowly circumstances*, it seems surreal that a Messiah of such stature would be born in the way He was! But all this is part of God's plan for redemption.

Look at the sovereignty of God at work. God used the frailty of the human institution of marriage to highlight the complexity of our human condition. It would appear that in reading these two verses that all we can see is drama: A young couple is pledged to be married. But lo and behold, the girl is pregnant. The marriage was about to end before it started.

Yet, how many of us know that even though we go through significant stress in our human relationships, and even though we have to endure twisted circumstances of fate, God in heaven is not caught off guard?

Just consider this clause: "*Before* they came together, she was found to be pregnant." Joseph is uncertain about his pledged wife's fidelity. He isn't too sure that she was faithful. But, thankfully, *God* is not deterred by this.

Actually, I'm glad that this story wasn't narrated with a husband and wife who perfectly loved one another, and then they came together one day and then they started a family without any fanfare. That's the sanitized fairy tale that we would create. The reality is so much better for our world.

Even the coming of the Messiah—into the world He created—was reported by Matthew in a way that one would usually associate with sin, hardship, mistrust, and hopelessness. Even the birth of the Messiah was not impervious to chaotic circumstances. So what makes you and me think that we can avoid them in this life? We can't! A fairy-tale version of this story could not intersect our lives in this way. But we thank God for choosing to come down through forty-two generations to us in Christ. We thank Him for entering into our world and in a manner that is highly relatable.

You might know the story of the young couple who went on a honeymoon on a cruise ship. While on the honeymoon, a terrific squall arose and beat upon the ship, knocking it to and fro. The man and his young wife were at the bow of this boat, and the boat began to lift quite heavily. They were uncertain of their fate, so they began to tell each other how much they loved each other; they began to share their regrets that they wouldn't be able to spend their lives together. They were certain that they would die in each other's arms.

The wife was so concerned that she called the captain of the ship and asked the captain, "Are we gonna die? Are we going down with this ship?" The experienced captain replied, "Ma'am, with all due respect, I need you to calm down; I need you to get a hold of yourself. You see, this ship was built with this storm in mind. So what I want you to do is lie down and go to sleep."

The chaos of this world, like a teen pregnancy, must concede to the sovereignty of God. He built us with the storms of life in mind. When we grasp that we are the recipients of His goodness, as in the case of our Messiah, goodness can come amidst complex human relationships. Hang in there, child of God; this may be a dark chapter in your life, but the Light of the World was born in Bethlehem!

The second way we see Jesus help us is by noting that God the Holy Spirit ensures us that all things are possible. God will send whatever or whomever is necessary to ensure that Joseph makes the right decision. In essence, the Holy Spirit of God says, "Who Mary is carrying is far more important than the creative way God has chosen to bring it to pass!" The Holy Spirit commenced this pregnancy, and the baby is He whom the Law and the prophets have been talking about. Sometimes we need this sort of reminder of God's power.

When chaos unleashes and setbacks cause us to cave in, we usually always want to blame the devil or point the finger at someone else. However, God may be enlarging your capacity to trust Him. God sends His Holy Spirit to enable us to endure. This angel is a messenger of God who was sent at the most strategic time to ensure Joseph that Mary would bear a son and that this Son would save humanity.

This text reminds you that no matter the circumstances, no matter the shame, God's Holy Spirit can enable and ensure you that all things are possible. And because Joseph yielded to the will of God, Joseph will name this boy. Joseph ultimately will give Him a divine name that reflects the mission of God: "He will save his people from their sins."

## Close

Yes,

> There is a Name I love to hear,
> I love to sing its worth;
> It sounds like music in my ear,
> The sweetest Name on earth.
>
> Oh, how I love Jesus,
> Oh, how I love Jesus,
> Oh, how I love Jesus,
> Because He first loved me![6]

---

6. Frederick Whitfield, "Oh How I Love Jesus" (1855), Timeless Truths, https://library.timelesstruths.org/music/Oh_How_I_Love_Jesus/.

Bless that wonderful name of Jesus.
Bless that wonderful name of Jesus.
Bless that wonderful name of Jesus.[7]

It is the name of the friend, who in your chaos, will see you through.

## CONCLUSION

I preached this sermon the last Sunday before Christmas. I used this message that morning so I could prepare another message that would pertain to Christmas Day. It is difficult to preach "Christmas" a Sunday before Christmas, or any Sunday of the year except Christmas Day itself, even though the story has implications for every day of the year! The expectation of the audience to hear a "Christmas message" on Christmas Day creates this difficulty.

Moreover, to ignore the teen pregnancy of Mary in an African American context would be quite insensitive. To demonstrate that the Lord used a pregnant, unwed, teen girl for His glory can provide hope for so many who have experienced the pain of such a situation in their families.

Finally, if one places the focus on the chaos of the pregnancy, one might be wise to push the final responses of Joseph into the background. Yet, one could also show that Joseph offers a response of grace—a response much needed when a teen girl reveals a pregnancy.

7. "Bless That Wonderful Name of Jesus," https://hymnary.org/text/theres_power_in_the_name_of_jesus_power.

# PART 2

# BIBLICAL EXPOSITION OF THE OLD TESTAMENT

# ENOUGH IS ENOUGH

*Expository Preaching from an Old Testament Pentateuch Book*

## DEUTERONOMY 1:1–8

### GEORGE PARKS JR.

This sermon was preached the last Sunday of 2018 at New Hope Baptist Church. The last Sunday of the year does not hold high liturgical or theological significance for the African American church, but it is significant in that God has been gracious in allowing us to make it another year. The last Sunday of the year in many African American church contexts provides a safe space for the preacher and ministry partners to look back in reflection and look forward with a renewed focus and commitment. Often, the closing of the year for many people, organizations, and churches is a time of evaluation. So often, many of us close a year, season, quarter, or a semester realizing we have not reached our goals or full potential, which sets the stage for a "holy discontent." That is a theme we find in Deuteronomy 1:1–8.

Because Deuteronomy 1:9–18 turns to the topic of appointing leaders, it was easy to separate 1:1–8 as its own pericope for preaching. Moreover, the contrast between "eleven days" and the "fortieth year," and the repeated emphasis on the land and taking possession of the land allows one to discern quickly that the focal point of the sermon concerns leaving the mountain (past) to take the land (future).

"You have stayed long enough at this mountain" (v. 6) provides the impetus for the title of this message: "Enough Is Enough." The title recognizes that the Lord has called it quits for Israel on resting in the wilderness—the place of disobedience. The book of Deuteronomy highlights the transition of Israel geographically, emotionally, and, above all, spiritually. Navigating transitions is a reality for maturing Christians, organizations, and churches. This text has significant possibilities for preaching, as it applicably relates especially to how local church bodies navigate transitions.

I believe clarity should be a relentless aim of the preacher in Sunday morning preaching. The sin of many messages is that they are good but unclear. Each week, I offer a Take Home Truth and a Deed to Do Statement. A truth to take home from this passage will be that God expects us to stop being satisfied with survival when abundance is available. On the basis of that truth, a deed to do in response to this passage will be to cease counterproductive thinking and behaviors and move with divine determination. Both the take home truth and deed to do will recur as ideas in the message.

## INTRODUCTION

"Enough is enough" is that potent expression that typically is interjected during a critical and intense moment. The phrase simply means, "What has been transpiring needs to cease," or "There is a needed shift from the status quo." It conveys frustration, even exasperation.

Maybe you've heard these words from a concerned matriarch of a family when two of her offspring have been estranged. The socially astute journalist that is supposed to maintain a neutral position writes "Enough is enough" when there is an obvious and heinous injustice discovered in a story. "Enough is enough" is what the instructor shouts to the students who persistently get off task and disrupt the educational process. "Enough is enough" was the attitude of our soul sister Fannie Lou Hamer when she said, "I'm sick and tired of being sick and tired," when she surveyed the conditions of black people being constantly marginalized. The phrase should be the words that fall from our lips when we notice the vulnerable being taken advantage of by the privileged.

"Enough is enough" is what you should say to yourself when you look at your life and you discover you are the culprit causing chaos! Sometimes we become stuck in mediocrity and our messes, parked in purposeless matters. Sometimes there is a muzzle on our mouths that leaves us unable to speak a word of progress over our own situation. Do you ever find yourself in the position of neutral? You're not going forward, neither are you going backward. But you're in a position to go either way. "Enough is enough!"

A symptom of Christian maturity is when we can become the foremen and project managers of our continued success: We must shout, monitor, strategize, and motivate ourselves to keep moving and pushing. However, there are difficult times and seasons that we find ourselves overcome with a form of spiritual laryngitis that leaves us unable to speak a word of motivation over our own existence. It is then, too, that we will be encouraged by the words of Deuteronomy 1 to hear from Moses's dealing with the Israelites that *enough is enough.*

In our text, Israel is a people emancipated from Egypt. They are en route to their promised land previously surveyed by twelve spies. They are a free people who yet maintained many slave habits. What an unfortunate reality it is for them that the chains from their wrist and ankles are loosed but their minds are still restricted. It is one thing to be free physically and legally; however, it requires another level of intentionality to rid ourselves of a slave mentality and practices. This new generation of people is struggling with the freedom that was first granted to their parents. Their leader, Moses, recounts for them when the Lord said enough is enough. It is time to go forward.

The book of Deuteronomy captures the transition of a new generation to the Promised Land from the journey in the wilderness. Not all the people who left Egypt made it to the edge of the Promised Land. Only Caleb, Joshua, Moses, and those under the age of sixty years old.[1] They are a people whom God is now moving to a place of great wealth, to a land "flowing with milk and honey" (Ex. 3:8). They are trading in a nomadic lifestyle for settled one, exchanging tents for houses. Their diet has changed from a wilderness diet to milk, honey, and the fruit of the land. This new generation of Israelites stands on the eve of their own reconstruction, preparing to cross into their promised place.

---

1. In Num. 14:28–30, the number of those entering the Promised Land was limited due to the sins of the people: "Say to them, 'As I live, declares the LORD, what you have said in my hearing I will do to you: your dead bodies shall fall in this wilderness, and of all your number, listed in the census from twenty years old and upward, who have grumbled against me, not one shall come into the land where I swore that I would make you dwell, except Caleb the son of Jephunneh and Joshua the son of Nun'" (ESV).

Through Moses, God will challenge the transitioning people to thoughtful reflection and action so that they might capture the Promised Land, so that they might gain all that the Lord has for them in life. He will tell them three things to do in order to leave mediocrity, stagnation, and spiritual lethargy behind and say "Enough!" to these things: Measure your progress, consider your position, and live in God's promise.

### *Measure Your Progress (1:1–6)*

The children of Israel are in Arabah. Moses calls their attention to when God challenged their forefathers when they were camped out at Mount Horeb. The journey to God's preferred and promised place was only to be a 150-mile journey. If this route was taken alone, by foot or a group, it should have at best only taken a few days, yet it took them nearly forty years. Now we know without a doubt God is on their side because He had sustained and supported them.

They had been fed with heaven's food called manna. God made wardrobe fashion to stand still and their clothes did not wear out. God manifested Himself in miraculous and undeniable ways, undeniably showing His faithfulness to the people of Israel.

The question is, then, why did such a short journey take so long? Because Israel's spiritual condition affected all other areas of their life. Moses now reminds the present generation that they should have arrived at their preferred place by now. They should not find themselves repeating the unhealthy (un)spiritual habits of the previous generation that failed to receive the promises of God.

That's a word for someone who's been so close yet so far away from your next level, blessing, promotion, and growth—not because it's not ready, but because spiritually you're not ready. You are like Israel—not heeding the Word of the Lord, not trusting Him to conquer the land and secure the blessings He has promised you. If we are not careful, our lives can mimic that of Israel, a people who have missed greatness more than once.

Measure your past progress and see if you have made your own 150-mile journey in eleven days or forty years, so to speak. What has slowed down your journey? Is it always something external on which you can place blame and free yourself of responsibility for your life situation? Or will an honest look reveal slackness in depending upon the Lord? Say to yourself, "Enough is enough!"

Anytime there is a lack of faithfulness to God on our part, progress will always be shorted. The children of Israel didn't have a strength or sophistication issue; they had spiritual and fidelity inconsistencies. That's a word for you who have great gifts, talents, connections, education, determination, and sophistication, but you're spiritually anorexic. Remember, "'Not by might nor by power, but by my Spirit,' says the Lord Almighty" (Zech. 4:6). Stop letting unspiritual habits continue to close the door on a better tomorrow; stop placing the blame on satanic forces when in reality it's our inner man that has wreaked havoc on our existence.

As believers, we cannot afford to buy into the erroneous thinking that our spirituality has no bearing on one's quality of life. Going part-time with our spiritual disciplines, diligence in service, personal worship, or love of our neighbor does not result in sustainable blessings. Our spiritual depth, in grace, will reflect itself in our life successes. In some sense, we fail to reach great heights because we have an unnurtured spirituality. We should, instead, nurture our spirituality as we nurture our marriages, parenting, social relationships, financial portfolio, and attire. Say to yourself, "Enough is enough."

### *Consider Your Position (1:6)*

Horeb was a dry, mountainous, parched, and burnt region. It was a place of trackless trails and limited resources. The children of Israel were in the wilderness. Their address might as well have been 222 Wilderness Lane, Wilderness City, TW (The Wilderness). There is no GPS system that could guide you to this place; *yet many of us know where this place is.*

Despite their location—or maybe because of their location—God had done some great things on their behalf. The Lord revealed Himself in power and glory. He gave the Ten Commandments to Moses to give to the people. The tabernacle was erected as a place of worship and to house the ark of the covenant—the place of God's presence. And the Levitical priesthood had been established to serve the Lord on behalf of God's people—to mediate the blessings of God.

All of these wonderful things took place in Horeb. God Himself made life in the wilderness livable. God provided these amenities, if you will, while Israel was disobedient. That is grace; that is mercy. Finally, however, God told them that they had stayed there long enough. The audacity of God is simply unnerving with this assessment. God always wants to push us out of our comfort zones of disobedience and toward more obedience.

God is urging them toward a productive place and away from the parched place for which they had settled, in part, because God had provided for them there in mercy. But it was God's mercy in the midst of their faithlessness. The Lord never intended the wilderness to be the place where they would retire. We must be able to discern that just because God has done something great in a place in the past doesn't necessarily mean that He wants us to stay there. We must remember that the death of Christ and His resurrection for us calls us to live all of life a new way (see Rom. 12:1–2; Eph. 4:17–24; 2 Cor. 5:17–18). We are new in Him, and we live in a new manner in Him by His power.

Often, we use our past as the only indication of what God can do. We then set that in concrete, when in fact God is being more progressive than we are. We never should place God in a box, and we definitively should not close the lid as if we know all of the ways of God.

We are tempted to fall in love with what God has done in the past, so much that we become handcuffed to it. God told the previous generation of Israelites, "Do not settle for the wilderness when I have greener pastures for you. Enough is enough: Let's move on from Wilderness Lane." Jesus and His inner circle—Peter, James, and John—were on the mountain when Jesus revealed Himself transfigured. What a beautiful sight it must have been to behold. Peter in his clumsy and unperceptive excitement responded to Jesus: let's stay on this mountain and build three tabernacles, one for Moses, one for Elijah, and one for you, Jesus. Peter wanted everyone to stay on that mountain. Jesus did not stay on that mountain as great as it was. You ask why? Because Jesus had an appointment on another mountain called Calvary. On that mountain He would secure our salvation. In the words of Dr. Marvin McMickle, "Do not find yourself celebrating on the wrong mountain." As Paul said in Philippians 3:12–13 (ESV), "Not that I have already obtained this or am already perfect, but I press on to make it my own, because Christ Jesus has made me his own. Brothers, I do not consider that I have made it my own. But one thing I do: forgetting what lies behind and straining forward to what lies ahead."

### Live in God's Promise (1:7–8)

God has big plans for this new generation. Moses must have been waiting with great anticipation for these people to finally get it!

Moses tells them to go and be actively intentional in securing the place that God has already provided. The people must move into action.

The people will not experience blessings in their hands until they moved their feet. Notice the areas they had to go: through the hill territory of Amorites, the Canaanites' lowland areas, Arabah encompassing the east and southeast area, and the Negev and the Euphrates River. Before they could enjoy promised territory, they had much work to do in the process. Even as we live by grace, we, like they, should stop expecting to experience great blessings absent of holy perspiration and godly determination.

The text says God swore the blessing to them. God

had sealed and bonded this agreement with the people. As this oral proclamation falls from the lips of God and flows through the mouth of Moses, there is a legal transfer of Israel's blessings to their children.

Imagine God has had a certificate of ownership of the Promised Land in His possession for forty years—a certificate that Israel could have obtained in a few days four decades ago. The envelope that was once crisp and white has, over time, become stained from the dust of delay and soiled from the wear of stubbornness. God tells this new generation that the contents of the worn envelop are still available!

I wonder how God feels when He has His promises ready for our seizing but is waiting on us. I suspect that a great many of our blessings are in Will Call, awaiting our pickup. Nevertheless, it is encouraging to know we serve a God who holds Himself accountable for keeping promises.

God promised to Abraham that his offspring would have occupation of the land. Several times in the book of Deuteronomy, God declares that He has given them the land. Enough with settling for the wilderness, believing you cannot do "X," or that you are disqualified because of past mistakes when God has given you promises based in His goodness. You can make it to a new place in life because you're walking with God's promise of love in hand. We do not know what the next month holds, let alone the next year! But we progress in life by holding on to God's promises.

"Paul reminds us in 2 Corinthians 1:20 (ESV), "For all the promises of God find their Yes in him. That is why it is through him that we utter our Amen to God for his Glory."

Some time ago, I was traveling back home from a preaching engagement. I left the plane to head to baggage claim to retrieve my luggage. To my surprise, it was not on the conveyer belt. My eyes wandered; there it was in the window of the luggage office. I went to retrieve my bag.

The attendant said, "Sir wait." I responded, "What do you mean?" She said, "Sir, how do you know it's your bag?" I said, "I know it's mine." She said, "Sir, do you have a claim ticket?" I said, "As a matter fact, I do!" I reached in my pocket showed her my claim ticket. She then turned to me a said," Here you go, sir; take your bag." God's Word today, for someone in my hearing, is for you to show your claim ticket—that is, for you to stand on the promises of God to bless you and be with you until you have secured all that He promises His children. Do not be afraid of what is before you. Enough is enough!

## CLOSE

As I close, I leave you with the words of Russell K. Carter:

Standing on the promises of Christ my king
Through eternal ages let His praises ring,
Glory in the highest, I will shout and sing,
Standing on the promises of God.

Standing on the promises that cannot fail,
When the howling storms of doubt and fear assail,
By the living Word of God I shall prevail,
Standing on the promises of God.

. . . . . . . . . . . . . . . . . . . . . . . .

Standing on the promises of Christ the Lord,
Bound to Him eternally by love's strong cord
Overcoming daily with the Spirit's sword,
Standing on the promises of God.

Standing on the promises I cannot fall,
List'ning every moment to the Spirit's call
Resting in my Savior as my all in all
Standing on the promises of God.

Standing, standing,
Standing on the promises of God my Savior;
Standing, standing,
I'm standing on the promises of God.[2]

## CONCLUSION

Our passage is the first in Moses's extended lecture series to the people. Moses reminds the people that God is a God who renews His covenant.[3] What a comforting word to people who received a promise, found themselves close to obtaining it, yet had not closed the deal on receiving their promise. We are offered insights of where the nation is located and how God has touched Moses to challenge the people.

A challenge of preaching this passage is to avoid allegorizing or spiritualizing the Promised Land, or reducing it to a type for heaven. The passage should not become a means to encourage

---

2. Russell K. Carter, "Standing on the Promises" (1886), Timeless Truths, https://library.timelesstruths.org/music/Standing_on_the_Promises/.

3. Paul House, *Old Testament Theology* (Downers Grove, IL: IVP, 1998), 169–70.

a local assembly to claim the promise of the land to Israel to be a promise for winning to Christ all of the souls in near proximity to the church. Neither should it encourage believers to strive for heaven, for salvation is by grace alone through faith alone in Christ alone; we do not strive for glory.

Finally, finding a place for the gospel in this sermon was not simple. The movement from old to new, however, allowed me to pick up on the theme of moving from one's old life to the fullness of one's new life in Christ.

# CHAPTER 5

# TAKE YOUR MOUNTAIN

*Expository Preaching from an*
*Old Testament Historical Book*

## JOSHUA 14:6–15
### ERIC C. REDMOND

This message was given for a Seniors' Day service at a gathering in Washington, DC. Finding an appropriate passage for senior saints about a senior saint in Scripture is a challenging task. One could draw from the significance of the words and acts of heroes of the faith in their older ages, such as Moses (Deut. 34), David (1 Kings 1), or Paul (2 Tim. 4). However, the meaning of Joshua 14:6–15 pertains to Caleb's age (v. 10), making the central idea of the passage the focus on Caleb's age—his *senior* age.

It was easy to separate 14:6–15 from the inheritance discussion in 14:1–5, for the focus turns to Caleb. The goal of the narrative is for Joshua to give Caleb the inheritance promised to him (see 14:9, 12). The failure at Kadesh-barnea, the length of the wandering in the wilderness, Caleb's age, and the presence of the Anakim all pose conflicts to prevent the goal from coming to fulfillment. However, Caleb's resolve to trust the Lord provides a resolution to the plot of the story (14:12, 14).

Both the NIV and ESV say, "Give me this hill country" (v. 12). But the KJV says, "Now therefore give me this mountain." The title, therefore, comes from what some would perceive to be the stronger picture of tackling a mountain rather than a hill. I also chose to follow the KJV knowing that many African American seniors of the WWII and Boomer generations would be sitting in front of me with a KJV and not an NIV or ESV Bible.

As with all sermons and passages of Scripture, important to this sermon is the challenging content to our modern worldview—specifically with respect to the ideas that achieving old age gives one the right to take life easy, and that senior saints are not beneficial to the growth of a church's ministry. On the latter, older believers often feel this way about themselves with respect to their local congregations. Ed Lewis writes of this worldview in his personal experience with a handful of older believers:

> I recently took time to ask a group of 10 respected older believers why they had difficulty with all the methods and changes in the church. **I asked what the major struggle is for them in seeing all these changes in the church.** Is it that the church is changing to reach younger adults? No. Is it because they do not like the music? They may not find it their choice but that is not the reason they struggle. Is it that the informal service is the issue? No. Is it that the church has gone to small groups instead of Sunday night services in most places? No. Is it that the preaching style has changed? No. Then what is it?
>
> They overwhelmingly stated that they struggle with the changes in the church because **they feel they are not needed . . . not included . . . overlooked . . . made to feel like they are "in the way."**[1]

1. Ed Lewis, "Keeping Old Adults in Church," *On Mission* blog, https://www.cenational.org/resource/keep-older-adults-church, accessed August 2, 2019.

Senior citizens feeling privileged to resign from working ministries in the church as they retire from the workforce or feeling pushed out of opportunities to serve meaningfully can result in a lack of older and mature workers serving in ministries in which they are most needed. High school and youth ministries need the wisdom of those who have reached the milestones that young, pimply-faced, immature adolescents can only dream of reaching. They need those in their late sixties, seventies, and eighties to tell them, "Make Choice A, not Choice B, for Choice A leads to happiness, blessing, prosperity, and life, while Choice B will harm and plague you well into your adult years." Teaching ministries of all types need people who have walked with the Lord for decades to tell those behind them of the Lord's faithfulness to His promises.

Now-retired pastor John Piper once said,

> Getting old to the glory of God means resolutely resisting the typical American dream of retirement. It means being so satisfied with all that God promises to be for us in Christ that we are set free from the cravings that create so much emptiness and uselessness in retirement. Instead, knowing that we have an infinitely satisfying and everlasting inheritance in God just over the horizon of life makes us zealous in our few remaining years here to spend ourselves in the sacrifices of love, not the accumulation of comforts.[2]

The story of Caleb models one aspect of living for the glory of God in one's old age. Caleb's life as a senior consists of more than reminiscing on the better days of the past, complaining about the

---

2. John Piper, "Getting Old for the Glory of God," *Desiring God*, https://www .desiringgod.org/messages/getting-old-for-the-glory-of-god, accessed August 2, 2019.

rate of technological changes in the church and society, or being nostalgic about a church's previous pastor. It holds out more for seniors than being resistant to change, enjoying material success, avoiding or embracing health challenges, and walking away from the church.[3] Preaching this passage will be very useful to helping an entire congregation begin rethinking what it means to live for the Lord as one's golden years arrive.

## INTRODUCTION

It certainly is a blessing to be a senior member of society. For many of you, it means you have survived the Great Depression, and watched as nine students attempted to integrate an Arkansas high school. You have lived through the assassination of the Kennedys and Dr. King, and you have seen the capture of Saddam Hussein and Osama bin Laden. You have witnessed World War II, the Korean War, the Vietnam War, two Gulf Wars, two African American Secretaries of State, and an African American President.

You have lived through the Twist, Woodstock, Funk, Disco, Rap, Go-Go, and Hip-Hop, and a few of you still

---

3. I recognize that there are many health disparities between older African Americans and older white Americans, and the issues of "avoiding or embracing health challenges" is not intended to overlook the role of mental and physical abilities in making choices on how or even whether to serve within a congregation. Caleb is quite robust and active for a person of his age. However, Caleb also is a former slave, and acknowledging such gives the preacher another means of connecting a senior audience to a senior biblical personality, and a means of keeping a hearer from quickly dismissing Caleb's story on the basis that he did not have the challenges to health posed by a racially discriminatory society. For more on health disparities between African Americans and white Americans, see Tracy Wharton, Daphne C. Watkins, Jamie Mitchell, and Helen Kales, "Older, Church-Going African Americans' Attitudes and Expectations About Formal Depression Care," *Research on Aging* 40.1 (January 2018): 3–26.

have some of the Jackson Five and Temptations' 45s and LPs in your closets. You have gone from typewriters to tablets, and black-n-white consoles to flat screens that pipe in stuff that you have no business watching. *Still, it's a great thing to live a long time!*

Along with all of these feats, however, come some real challenges as the years pile on. First, you tend to become a bit more timid than you used to be. You don't drive as fast or with as much confidence as you used to. You are more concerned about the security of your money and wonder whether you have enough insurance to cover your needs until you leave this world. You are sure about Jesus. *You just aren't sure about yourselves.*

Second, you, unfortunately, begin to experience a loss of strength. Back in the day, you could go all day with basketball. Now some of you are good if you can roll both feet out of bed without creaking in all of your bones. One A Day vitamins and Centrum are important, but sometimes an extra arthritis pill just works better.

A third thing you face is that your will to fight diminishes. You just don't have time to argue endlessly anymore. You probably do not feel like marching for every initiative and running down to the city council to make things happen. That's what youth was for. Now you just want your kids and grandkids to be good to you, and for your young neighbors to turn down their music. If you could have that much, most of you would be good!

It is one thing for you, as elderly members of society, to perceive yourselves as timid, physically weaker, and not wishing to fight. You can accept that and adjust to it. However, it is another thing when these things are *imposed* upon you—when you lose a position that should be yours by seniority; when you are overlooked for gains that you know you can handle; or when someone takes advantage of your age and there seems to be no recourse for justice. And if all of that were not enough, some of you even feel pushed aside in the church!

I want to tell you that this is not the time to give in to timidity or low energy levels, or to give way to complacency that will not fight for what is yours. There is much more for God to give to you and to do through you. When the Lord is finished using you and all of your knowledge, experiences, skills, and training, He will call you home. In the meantime, you need to go against natural tendencies to slow down as seniors, and you need to act like Caleb and *go take your mountain.*

## Transition

You are familiar with the story here. Joshua is leading the children of God into the Promised Land—a land flowing with milk and honey. But God does not hand them the Promised Land. He tells them to go defeat the nations in Canaan and take the land from them. Contrary to popular church talk, God does not hand us everything on a silver platter in this life. In the next life He will. But here, some things require the use of the tools of this world, in the fear of God, to get what we need.

By this time, many of the twelve tribes have acquired their inheritances, but Caleb has not gotten what was due to him for bringing back a good report when he spied out the land. So, he wants his piece of the pie too. Really, what he wants is to do more for God, the God who delivered him from slavery in Egypt.

This is not going to be a small feat for Caleb. Caleb is not a young and spry forty-five-year-old anymore; remember, God took forty years dropping those disobedient Israelites in the wilderness. So Caleb is now eighty-five years old! This is an old man trying to get what belongs to him! This is a man with all the same frailties seniors have today. And his inheritance is in the hill country, not in the plains and valleys.

Caleb, however is not going to let this stop him from getting the mountain that belongs to him, and he's going to tell you how to get yours too.

## Remain Faithful While Others Are Faithless (vv. 7–9)

You remember what happened when Moses sent the twelve spies into the land. All of them searched around the land and saw the luscious fruit, fortified cities, and descendants of the giants. However, when they brought the report back, Joshua and Caleb interpreted the events differently. While the people saw huge obstacles to their inheritance, Caleb was one of two who said, "Let's go take the land!"

A good question to ask here might be, "What made the difference between the report of the two and the report of the ten?" Caleb tells us right here: *I wholly followed the Lord. I didn't follow Him until I got to obstacles I thought were bigger than I am. With God on my side, I know that I never look like a grasshopper in the sight of anybody!*

What he is saying to Joshua now is this: *I was faithful*

*then when the others were not, and I am still faithful now. If the hill country is my inheritance, then move out of the way so I can keep being faithful. I've got a mountain to go take.*

In the same way, many of you have been faithful in following the Lord to do great things when other believers were afraid to step out and believe God for the impossible. You would gather in prayer—sometimes all night if we had to! You would make sacrifices and trust that God would supply for all of your needs, even if you didn't fully understand the new vision the pastor was giving. Now, though, instead of living by faith, some of us need an *explanation* on everything in order to think about being faithful. And when you don't get it, instead of being faithful, you vote with your feet: You just stop showing up to events.

Now is not the time to draw back, become a gossiper, or have a perpetual pity party. If anything, the Lord wants *you* to be more faithful now than ever! Who else is going to show the younger generation how to live on a shoestring budget and still raise a family? Who else is going to pass on the wealth of knowledge needed to run the ministries you have been leading for twenty and thirty years? Who is going to show the Millennials how to stay on a job they don't like for more than five minutes? You! You, by your faithful service and by wholly following the Lord, can help a whole mixed-up generation learn how to be faithful to the Lord!

## Remain Strong When You Should Be Settled (vv. 10–11)

Caleb is not on some special medicine when he says he is just as strong at eighty-five as he was in his forties. Instead, his strength is up because he is strong *in the Lord*. On this passage, John Calvin says of Caleb, "He lays claim not only to the skill and valor of a leader, but also to the physical strength of a soldier."[4]

We should assume that Caleb, like Joshua, followed the book of the Law "day and night," doing according to all written therein (Josh. 1:8). We should assume that the words of the Lord made him strong and courageous, as it did Joshua. We should assume that he is still leading the armies of Israel in victory because he is increasing in his knowledge of the Lord!

I have no doubt that in all his wars, he had picked up some bumps and bruises, and was feeling pains in places he did not know previously existed. At eighty-five, he should be seeking retirement, trying to find a few bus trips to watch *A Raisin in the Sun* on Broadway, or go shopping in Lancaster or King of Prussia, Pennsylvania. He should be trying to figure out how to move from Canaan down to South Sinai so he can lower his living expenses and move back around family. But instead of settling and taking it easier, he is trying to do *more*. Caleb understands that in the Lord is he old, but he is not dead.

It is a thing for people today to say something like, "Sixty is the new forty," and "Seventy is the new fifty." I guess that means when you are eighty, you really have the body, mind, and strength of someone who is sixty!

The point of saying "Sixty is the new forty" is to say

4. John Calvin, *Commentaries on the Book of Joshua*, trans. Henry Beveridge (Grand Rapids: Christian Classics Ethereal Library, n.d.), 14:9, https://www .ccel.org/ccel/calvin/calcom07.xvii.i.html.

that modern healthcare and the emphasis on diet and exercise in our day has made a way for you to be as healthy and active today at sixty as previous generations were at forty. So when a church is full of sixty-plus-year-olds, it should not be stagnant! Instead, this new force of other forty- and fifty-year-olds should be leading us in witnessing on the street, pulling together discipleship groups to teach people the Scriptures, taking missions trips that those raising small children cannot do, and filling up the children and youth ministries with mentors, teachers, and activity developers!

Don't wait on someone else to do the ministry work and sit back and complain about how bad youth are today. Get in there and show the high school and middle school students how to live by exposing your life to them. Go beyond Sunday school and teach some young men how to develop a prayer life; teach some young ladies how to walk by the power of the Spirit. Don't just tell them to be modest; invite them to meet as a group in your home and then discuss modesty with them, show them how to be modest, tell them about your failure with modesty (and with your early relationships), and let them come to you without criticism when they are struggling.

This is not the time of life to sit down and wait to be served. "[Jesus] came not to be served but to serve, and to give his life as a ransom for many" (Mark 10:45)! You, Brother and Sister Senior Saint, need to follow your Lord and Caleb, stop talking about how you aren't as strong as you used to be, and get to serving in the most needy and difficult mountains in this church. *Go take your mountain!*

## Remain Courageous When There Are Enemies Left to Conquer (11–12)

Caleb could not have cared less about the size of the challenges before him. He does not care about the fact that he has to go into the hill country to get the inheritance. He is not concerned that the offspring of the Nephilim, the Anakim (the race of giants), are there. (Yes, the Bible records multiple times that the Anakim were like giants to the average man—probably what we would describe as seven feet tall since we know that even until the tenth century BC the average height of a grown man was less than five feet and three inches—a fact we know based on ancient coffin sizes and skeletal remains.) Giants were no matter to Caleb.

Neither did the fact that the cities were fortified bother him. Caleb understood that having the Lord with him made him have a majority. *With the Lord*, mountains were the same to him as plains; *with the Lord*, the Anakim were just people who were going to fall harder when they fell; *with the Lord*, fortified cities would crumble like Jericho, as if they were made of sticks—the big, good God wouldn't even have to "huff and puff' to blow their cities down! Caleb knew that no enemy is a match for our God.

So Caleb remained *courageous*. Changes on the block couldn't make him keep his blinds down and stay inside. People with big titles, fancy jobs, and lots of money couldn't keep him for standing up for right on a committee. Caleb would not have been afraid to look another man in the eye and tell him he needs to repent of living in sin.

Caleb would have stood up to anyone, and he would have put a stop to any secret meetings of people with private agendas trying to sway Israel to go in a certain direction—people not concerned about what the Bible says about leading God's people!

When you are staring down the face of the enemies of God, it is not time to quiver; it is time to be available for God to call you into action. This is especially true for we who have the Holy Spirit living in us—for we who believe that Jesus is going to raise us from the dead! How in the world do we think someone is going to raise our bodies from the dead if He can't give us the strength to look people in the eye when they are opposing His righteousness? Which one is harder? If you know that Jesus will raise you from the dead, then you should also know that He gives you the power to be courageous for His name's sake.

Not to mention, the courage of all our new non-chocolate neighbors in the city—many of whom don't go to church—shames us. They walk up and down these streets like they own them; they don't seem to be scared of anything. They are taking over, and changing the marriage laws in your city, and the gambling laws will soon follow! They establish yoga gyms, organic food stores, and one day (unfortunately, depending upon where the politics go), cannabis shops—right on the same corners where the drug dealers once stood. And what are we doing? We are getting in our cars, going back home, closing our doors and ignoring crime, poverty, and the need for better schools, when of all people we have real power and a real solution for every need in the city. But we are going to have to exercise some godly *courage* to go take these mountains.

## Close

When we start talking about taking mountains, many images come to mind. We think of people scaling Mt. Everest to kids playing "King of the Hill"; from Hannibal crossing the Alps to defeat the Romans to the monument to our Marines raising the American flag at the summit of Mt. Suribachi during the battle for Iwo Jima. Even from American folklore, we have John Henry tunneling through the mountain with his hammer in order to defeat the emerging technology of his day.

But when it comes to really taking a mountain, there never has been and never will be one like the mount called Calvary. For on that mountain Jesus, beaten and bruised, faced a strong enemy called Death. On that mountain, Jesus, wanting the cup to pass from Him, still took on your sin and my sin. On that mountain, Jesus, mocked and rejected, crowned with thorns and spat upon, bore the wrath of God that was due to each one of us. On that mountain, Jesus, with nails in His hands, hung, and with nails in His feet, bled. On that mountain Jesus died. Oh, He died! And three days after conquering that mountain, He got up with all power in His hands!

Jesus took the mountain of the cross of Calvary so that no challenge in this life would be too great for us! Senior, *go take your mountain*, just like Caleb, and just like Jesus!

## CONCLUSION

I did not necessarily run into a concern about the text of the message. However, I was concerned about the issue of credibility: The sermon would have had a greater impact if I were also a senior—with seniors as my audience. Knowing this, before I spoke, I removed some humor from my original draft, because I was not sure how it would be received from someone significantly younger than the audience. I am sure the humor would have been fine coming from another senior. But it was better for me to err on the side of caution rather than be perceived as being presumptuous or even arrogant.

I also had to avoid the temptation of reviewing Caleb's entire story. He is a less prominent character in Scripture, even though he was one of the two spies who brought back a favorable report about the Promised Land. I simply assumed the seniors' knowledge of Joshua and Caleb as spies, and assumed their general familiarity with the subject of the book of Joshua: the conquering of the land inheritance. To review Caleb's life might have bogged down the exposition or even obscured the central idea of the passage.

Additionally, I shortened the length of this sermon because of the nature of the service. Being a special afternoon service, I was aware that my audience would have sat through one or two morning worship services prior to returning to this afternoon service. If I were preaching Joshua 14 as part of a morning series, I could have lengthened this sermon, possibly even adding in the exposition of 14:1–5. However, it seemed wise to consider "less is more" when speaking to a largely senior audience in the afternoon when both they and I were tired.

Finally, because Caleb references taking a mountain, it was easy to make a beeline to the gospel. I wanted the seniors to understand that this passage is not promoting self-help or self-actualization. Instead, the strength to serve faithfully in one's old age comes from the power of the One who tackled the mount known to us as "Calvary." Jesus' death and resurrection provide the grace needed to be found faithful to Him, regardless of one's age, abilities, or challenges. It is important to proclaim the gospel, even to seniors who have been in church for a long time, for not all of them know the gospel or see its significance to all of life. One should not assume that length of stay in a church means clarity on the gospel, or that it means discipleship in the gospel.

# CHAPTER 6

# HOLLA IF YOU HEAR ME— THE MISSION OF WORSHIP

*Expository Preaching from an Old Testament Poetical Book*

## PSALM 96

## ERIC MASON

"Take your Bible and take your newspaper, and read both. But interpret newspapers from your Bible." Karl Barth[1]

In this sermon, I will use Psalm 96 as a springboard for aiding the preacher in formulating a biblical, Christ-centered, and relevant sermon from poetic material. Utilizing the rich figures of speech found in the text, we will see through the eyes of the human author the realities of an eternal God.

I preached this sermon to my congregation in North Philadelphia in a Sunday morning worship service. At the time of the preaching of this message, my congregation was filled with many

---

1. "Barth in Retirement," *Time Magazine*, May 31, 1963.

believers in their twenties and thirties, and I had a sprinkling of members comprised of older ages.

In this sermon, you will note the references to African American life, and such life in Philly in particular. Unashamedly, I am going to draw in the readers by giving visual images of Philly neighborhoods as-is and not of some polished picture that overlooks urban blight or portrays the relative cleanliness of the suburbs. Such a picture would not be helpful to my context, neither would it help my young folk see that the Lord is at work among our people in the city—even in the troubles of neighborhoods around us. As in traditional black preaching, I will not ignore or gloss-over what relates to the average African American experience. My exposition will not neglect speaking to reality in order to speak of God's offer of hope to us.

Moreover, the use of terms like "El Elyon" for God and "shalom meter" reflect the direct, rhetorical flare that speaks to our people. This is where African American exposition differs from exposition in the majority culture: We do not view the use of embellished language as "lofty speech" or arrogance, but as edifying identification coding. Our people are built up in their spirits when their spiritual leaders exercise tremendous command of the English language and make such language dance with unusual wordings and placements of words. Such use of words allows our people to see that the Lord speaks with the colorfulness with which we talk to one another, and not simply with what is perceived to be sterile, academic language used by some of our counterparts of other hues.

In a similar way, references to Hip-Hop culture and the closing song are things that say to an African American congregation, "This is the Word of God for *you*." I attempt to walk through the riches of Psalm 96 as an African American pastor speaking to an

African American people about the majesty of the God who loves them and intends to reach all peoples.

## INTRODUCTION

Every Tuesday, I get out in the neighborhood of Epiphany Fellowship Church early for a time of worshipful engagement with Yahweh as I walk, drive, and or bike the neighborhood. No matter the weather, I am out on the block. Alone, I engage with God as I observe the state of affairs in the neighborhood. I look at the dilapidated structures, broken economy, drug issues, gentrification, public housing, kids going to school, fathers and mothers walking children to school, homeless people looking for a meal and a quarter, blue-collared workers going to work, construction workers rehabbing properties, and the number of churches that riddle 100-year-old edifices and dilapidated storefronts. I see the murals, graffiti, trash, cornerstones, and a history of vibrancy yet gone and to be rediscovered, and I'm talking to *El Elyon* about the picture of what it could be if the kingdom came to North Philly.

At times, I'm weighed down, and other times I'm encouraged by the wind of the Spirit for my city. My dreaming eye is like Paul's in Athens as I see the gap between the community's deep brokenness and its need for regeneration and Jesus' transformative healing to make it comprehensively whole. In Acts 17:16, we read that Paul "was deeply distressed when he saw that the city was full of idols. "Deeply distressed" means to be provoked or to be or become incited or stirred up in one's emotions, feelings, or reactions. It can be positive or negative. It also can mean to be upset, angered, irritated, distressed,[2] or to let oneself be carried away (in anger), or to get excited.[3]

At the heart of worship in preaching is the impassioned desire of the preacher for the nations to worship Yahweh. This passion doesn't start in the pulpit but on the pavement. In essence, this great quote sums it up well:

> Missions is not the ultimate goal of the church. Worship is. Missions exists because worship doesn't. Worship is ultimate, not missions, because God is ultimate, not man.[4]

In light of this, my shalom meter is high, wanting for the gospel to fill the gaps of brokenness that exist because of the fall. Psalm 96 is a great measure of where we are in the process of the visionary prowess of the eternal God for the nations to worship. Worship in the gathering led by Christ-centered, covenant songs that motivate missiological engagement of the nations by the people of God for all times.

*Worship is designed to exalt the essence of God, edify the souls of the redeemed, and evangelize the lost.* "Sing to the LORD a new song" says the psalmist! Several times the Old Testament records the creation of *new* music. This was common after military victories (see Ex. 15:1; Judg. 5:1; 1 Sam. 18:6–7). When the ark was brought to Jerusalem,

---

2. J. Swanson, *Dictionary of Biblical Languages with Semantic Domains: Greek (New Testament)* (Oak Harbor, OH: Logos Research Systems, Inc., 1997).

3. H. R. Balz and G. Schneider, *Exegetical Dictionary of the New Testament*, vol. 3 (Grand Rapids: Eerdmans Publishing Co., 1990), 43.

4. John Piper, *Let the Nations Be Glad! The Supremacy of God in Missions*, 2nd ed. (Grand Rapids: Baker Academic, 2010), 17.

David commissioned a new song (1 Chron. 16:7). Psalm 96, or at least its first edition, originated from this commissioning context, which one sees readily by comparing Psalm 96 with 1 Chronicles 16:23–33. Any fresh experience of God may offer an occasion for the composition of a "new song."[5] New songs were for new and fresh experiences with God in the world flowing from rich gatherings of the saints.

In preaching such a Psalm, one must have this in mind that Psalms 96–99 point to the appetite of the believer in the world for Yahweh to reign. Worship is the mechanism to engage the soul in this deep longing that was placed in us by Yahweh. Singing to Yahweh always leads to somewhere, and for us that somewhere is proclamation and mission in the world.

Note the series of six imperatives: *sing—sing—sing—bless—proclaim—declare*. The threefold use of שׁירו, "sing," is impressive, followed by the verbs בשׂר and ספר in verses 2 and 3. The verb בשׂר carries the idea of "bringing news/a message," which involves "good news" in the Old Testament (one exception seems to be the use of the word מבשׂר, "messenger," in 1 Sam. 4:17 KJV).[6] Its use in the proclamation of Yahweh's saving acts is appropriate in Psalm 96 (see also Isa. 40:9; 41:27; 52:7; 60:6; 61:1; Nah. 1:2).[7]

---

5. J. H. Walton, *Zondervan Illustrated Bible Backgrounds Commentary (Old Testament): The Minor Prophets, Job, Psalms, Proverbs, Ecclesiastes, Song of Songs*, vol. 5 (Grand Rapids: Zondervan, 2009), 402.

6. See *TDOT*, III, 314.

7. Marvin E. Tate, M.E., *Psalms 51–100* (Dallas: Word, Inc., 1998), 512.

Our worship is a call to represent our God in the world. *Preaching must be worship.* Worship-less preaching is boring preaching, but worshipful preaching is fiery and inspirational. Although Israel was a somewhat closed community, it was never meant to stay that way. The worship leaders and preachers were to be emcees, or rather, MCs of a grand worship service. In Hip-Hop, "MC" doesn't mean "Master of Ceremony" but "move the crowd." To make it plain, worshipful preaching is to be an intellectual, emotional, and volitional movement.

Show me the text! Why should I sing? Verse 4 (CSB) says, "For the LORD is great and is highly praised." As the psalm gives reasons for the Lord to be praised, it speaks, "He is to be feared above all gods." These words journey back to Deuteronomy 32:8–9, verses that Michael Heiser calls the Deuteronomy 32 worldview: "When the Most High gave the nations their inheritance and divided the human race, he set the boundaries of the peoples according to the number of the people of Israel. But the LORD's portion is his people, Jacob, his own inheritance" (Deut. 32:8–9 CSB).

The nations rejected Yahweh as their God, and He disinherited the nations and divided them amongst the sons of Elohim. Israel was supposed to rule the nations justly under the rule of Yahweh. However, in Psalm 82:1–2, God pronounces His judgment upon the sons of God in light of their rebellion in Genesis 6. By leading nations to rebel through invoking evil and wanting power they functionally broke with the living God and stood in judgment. However, God desires to re-inherit the nations. In re-inheriting the nations, Israel was the original royal priesthood to call the nations back to Yahweh.

As we read the psalm, we see the duty of Israel: to sing, bless, and proclaim the works of God among the nations. God wants representatives from all nations to be taught the ways of Yahweh through proclamation and songs as they are engaged by the covenant community. *Proclaim His salvation. . . . Declare His glory among the nations, His wondrous works among all the peoples.*

In addition, Israel's duty was to abandon their false gods and return to Yahweh. As redemptive history tells it, Israel refused to fully live up to their missionary call over and over again. Yet, the Lord still held Israel accountable to their missionary call: "Now if you will carefully listen to me and keep my covenant, you will be *my own posses-sion out of all the peoples, although the whole earth is mine,* and you will *be my kingdom of priests* and *my holy nation.'* These are the words that you are to say to the Israelites" (Ex. 19:5–6 CSB, emphasis added).

As a cultic worshiping community, they were to know God and His ways, and they were to engage the world, tell-ing the nations about who God is through their identity as worshipers. Mission to the lost was to be the outcome of their worship. Intellectually, they were to be clear on who God is and what their purpose was. Emotionally, they were to have their affections for God stirred because of what they were taught from His law. (Singing and fiery wor-ship must follow such knowledge.) Volitionally, they were called to do something about what they learned and came to know. Good preaching makes this movement.

## Christ in Psalm 96

Where is Jesus in all this? In speaking of God as King in these psalms, we discover that Jesus is the fulfillment and incarnation of God the King. Jesus will rule as Davidic King on behalf of the Godhead over the nations. The Psalm says, "Say among the nations: 'The LORD reigns. The world is firmly established; it cannot be shaken. He judges the peoples fairly'" (Ps. 96:10 CSB). Jesus declares in John 5:22–23 (CSB), "The Father, in fact, judges no one but has given all judgment to the Son, so that all people may honor the Son just as they honor the Father. Anyone who does not honor the Son does not honor the Father who sent him." Judgment here involves governing, including bringing justice—"deciding what is right and wrong, implying" also "a punishment or reward to follow, and usually according to an agreed set of principles."[8] It also involves formally giving a judge the power to punish or reward.[9] The term is rich! Jesus will bring comprehensive *justice*. His justice concerns not only Israel, but also, in this context, the entire world (for example, "Let the *nations* be glad!" Ps. 67:4 (NASB, ESV, KJV).

In our contemporary times, in which minorities often are denied justice and where leadership lacks moral fiber, Jesus remains both moral in character and clear in the ways of Yahweh. As Jesus in His earthly ministry gave Israel chances to repent and turn to Him as the true Israel, they also would be given the chance to live up to their calling

---

8. James A. Swanson, *Dictionary of Biblical Languages with Semantic Domains: Hebrew (OT)* (Bellingham, WA: Faithlife, 1997).

9. Ibid.

through Him. However, Jesus didn't limit the extent of His ministry to Israel, but gave a commission to go to the nations instead of waiting for the nations to come to Israel. Jesus commissions His disciples to call the nations to the repentance that Israel didn't have and didn't proclaim. Now we have a newer song in Jesus!

Where Israel failed, Jesus is victor. Now He inaugurates the beginning of one new humanity through His cross and resurrection, for both Jew and Gentile to gather from the nations as an elect community. In Jesus, Yahweh re-inherits for Himself all people to Himself by faith in Jesus. Now the kingdom of priests will be both Jews and Gentiles. Peter picks up this concept: "But you are a chosen race, a royal priesthood, a holy nation, a people for his possession, so that you may proclaim the praises of the one who called you out of darkness into his marvelous light. Once you were not a people, but now you are God's people; you had not received mercy, but now you have received mercy" (1 Peter 2:9–10 csb).

In urban neighborhoods, many black Hebrew Israelites claim that they are the only elect people. They are like modern Judaizers who limit God's reign to themselves alone. Although some of them would say Gentiles will come in to God's kingdom, others say Gentiles, nations, and peoples are scattered Israelites yet to be awakened.

Yahweh's covenant plan always included the nations. The church is the new humanity made of both Jews and Gentiles. Proclaiming anything less than this is another gospel and damnable.

The church is now tasked with what Israel as a whole has failed to accomplish. Our worship and preaching should lead us into the broken and forgotten places where people need to hear the name of the Lord. It should lead us into places where many would not dare to go: to the urban and rural housing projects and forsaken cul-de-sacs, to the block, to the boardroom, to the grocery stores and corner stores; to neighborhoods with Whole Foods, and places where there is only soul food; to prisons, to unknown tribes, to united nations and unknown nations, to places where the souls of the lost might have their life questions answered by the gospel! Our singing should be filled with vamps, hymnal theology, vast instrumentation, and every redeemable genre of music that we can use to sing of God's praises to the peoples of the world! Our God demands this of us! And then one day, we will all worship at the throne of the eternal King where the chosen from every tribe and tongue make their way because of the blood of the Lamb and the word of His testimony. As I say at the end of *Woke Church*,

> If the church can keep this image of what is to come before us, we will be energized to work to accomplish His purposes in the earth. We will work as one unified body, across all ethnic lines. When the Philadelphia Eagles won the Super Bowl, people in the city of Philadelphia flooded the streets. There was a celebration like never before. They were all wearing one jersey: the Eagles team jersey. Philly is a very racially divided city, from Little Italy, to the Black Sunni Salafee orthodox Muslims of 52nd Street, to the Chinese in China Town. However, on that day, everyone—almost one million people—forgot their differences and flooded the streets of Philadelphia. They forgot about all of their differences and all of their frustrations, because

the ones who had won the game represented all of the people of Philly. Instead of fighting each other, they gathered around the ones who won the game for them, forgetting that they ever had differences.

When Jesus returns, the global multiethnic church will have on the same white jersey. We will put away our differences and with one voice will shout together, "Salvation belongs to our God, who is seated on the throne, and to the Lamb!" (Rev. 7:10). "Hallelujah! Salvation, glory, and power belong to our God, because his judgments are true and righteous, because he has judged the notorious prostitute who corrupted the earth with her sexual immorality; and he has avenged the blood of his servants that was on her hands."[10]

## Close

Sing a new song to the LORD;
let the whole earth sing to the LORD.
Sing to the LORD, bless his name;
proclaim his salvation from day to day.
Declare his glory among the nations,
his wondrous works among all peoples.

For the LORD is great and is highly praised;
he is feared above all gods.
For all the gods of the peoples are idols,
but the LORD made the heavens.
Splendor and majesty are before him;
strength and beauty are in his sanctuary.

---

10. Eric Mason, *Woke Church: An Urgent Call for Christians in America to Confront Racism and Injustice* (Chicago: Moody Publishers, 2018), 180–81.

Ascribe to the LORD, you families of the peoples,
ascribe to the LORD glory and strength.
Ascribe to the LORD the glory of his name;
bring an offering and enter his courts.
Worship the LORD in the splendor of his holiness;
let the whole earth tremble before him.

Say among the nations: "The LORD reigns.
The world is firmly established; it cannot be shaken.
He judges the peoples fairly."
Let the heavens be glad and the earth rejoice;
let the sea and all that fills it resound.
Let the fields and everything in them celebrate.
Then all the trees of the forest will shout for joy
before the LORD, for he is coming—
for he is coming to judge the earth.
He will judge the world with righteousness
and the peoples with his faithfulness. (Ps. 96:1–13 CSB)

## CONCLUSION

After reviewing the preached sermon, two challenges were evident. First, I make this statement early in the sermon: "At the heart of worship in preaching is the impassioned desire of the preacher for the nations to worship Yahweh. This passion doesn't start in the pulpit but on the pavement." In doing so, I am focusing on the urban neighborhoods of Philadelphia as a subset of "the nations." It is on Philadelphia's "pavement" that I am challenging my people to proclaim the greatness of God so that He might be worshiped in our city.

However, "the nations" properly refer to anyone outside of ethnic Israel, and the New Testament writers recognize all people groups of the earth under the concept of nations (for example, Matt. 28:19–20). While I repeated that the Lord wants all of earth to worship Him, if I had pointed to an example of our church's support of African Americans involved in missions work among people groups outside of the US, I would have demonstrated that more than Philly is in view in this psalm. The emphasis on Philadelphia is consistent with the history of African American preaching that focuses on the immediate and tangible rather than ignoring social realities on American soil. An example of African American missions involvement would have been a bonus.

Second, due to Sunday morning time limitations, I could discuss Psalm 96:1–9 only broadly. However, this passage deserves a second sermon (or simply a longer one!) in which the focus on the nations' worship gives way to the cosmic and eschatological worship of 96:10–13. Psalm 96 goes beyond the people of the earth worshiping to a picture of a renewed creation bringing glory to her Creator (see Rom. 8:19–24). In such a sermon, I could explain the magnificence of God to which the figures of seas roaring, fields exalting, and trees singing point. I would also show that worship of God results in being faithful to Him—a faithfulness He will come to judge when He returns to renew all things. Such discussions would naturally include presenting a theological view on the ends times; it would allow me to say that our view on the end times matters to our worship and mission in the present age.

CHAPTER 7

# THE MINISTRY OF VISION

*Expository Preaching from an Old Testament Prophetic Book, Largely Poetical*

## HABAKKUK 2:1–4
## TERRY D. STREETER

In 2005, I preached a sermon series from the book of Habakkuk at Mount Pleasant Baptist Church in Washington, DC, where I have served as the Senior Pastor for thirty years. The original version of the sermon in this chapter was preached in that series.

A church business meeting was approaching where I would present my vision for the church. I wanted the church to have a biblical understanding of vision—what it is and how it would help us. This sermon was my way of preparing the people for the presentation of my vision by letting them see the ministry of vision through the eyes of Habakkuk. Habakkuk's encounter with God gave the people a clear view of the importance of vision in planning the future of the church.

This sermon was well received by the congregation. It led to my teaching a workshop on leadership and vision casting. I was also invited to facilitate leadership training workshops at other churches, explaining vision casting through an expository walk in the biblical text.

My challenge when preaching this sermon in its original form, and the subsequent revisions, was finding an appropriate application of the message that remained true to the Scripture's core message, yet relevant to present day situations in the lives of the hearers. It is what I call getting to the "so what?" of the sermon. The impact of the biblical text is great when people can see their own life condition in the text. The people were able to not just understand the vision for the church, but they were able to envision the transforming power of vision in their own lives. They fully understand why the people perish where there is no vision.

## INTRODUCTION

> "I will stand upon my watch, and set me upon the tower, and will watch to see what he will say unto me, and what I shall answer when I am reproved. And the LORD answered me, and said, Write the vision, and make it plain upon tables, that he may run that readeth it. For the vision is yet for an appointed time, but at the end it shall speak, and not lie: though it tarry, wait for it; because it will surely come, it will not tarry. Behold, his soul which is lifted up is not upright in him: but the just shall live by his faith." (Hab. 2:1–4 KJV)[1]

Proverbs 29:18 declares, "Where there is no vision, the people perish." This is what the prophet shows us in Habakkuk 2:1–4. Judah is perishing because of immorality and evil throughout the nation. Habakkuk does not

---

1. The KJV is used throughout this chapter unless noted otherwise.

understand why God hasn't given him a message of condemnation and punishment to deliver to this perverse generation. God is silent. In torment, the prophet cries out his complaints to God. Finally, God lets him know His plan to rectify the situation by allowing Babylon to plunder and capture Judah in war.

Now Habakkuk is truly distressed. Would God *really* use a nation more wicked than Judah to correct Judah? Habakkuk was asking God, "Do You know what You are doing?" Keep in mind that we are speaking of God's chosen people. How could God use a wicked nation to judge His chosen people? The prophet is disturbed because God seems unconcerned about Judah's plight. Habakkuk sees the Chaldeans as a destructive force that devoured nations like one crushes a bug. So, how long will God allow this to continue?

Interestingly, many of us who have difficulty with God never slow down long enough to wait on His answer. We are impatient and feel that if God doesn't answer immediately that God will never answer. That is far from the truth. Habakkuk is patient and waits for God's answer. God does answer and tells him what to do with the vision. The Hebrew word here for "vision" is *chazah*, a word that means "a mental sight, a revelation, an oracle or prophesy." Habakkuk's answer comes as a vision or revelation. Our text demonstrates how we are to handle our vision.

While so many of us speak fondly of the good old days when things were not as they are now, we cannot live life looking backwards. What God did then, and how God did it then, might not be what God wants to do in this present age. When there is no vision, people do find themselves tied to the past traditions, because that is what they know or have seen. Visions look to the future and make plain our path. Habakkuk is given a vision. God's instructions to him are a lesson for us all on how to deal with our vision. If our churches are to survive, we must have a vision and know how to handle that vision. There are five things that are clearly seen in this text regarding having and working with our vision.

## Vision Comes from God (2:1)

"I will stand upon my watch, and set me upon the tower, and will watch to see what he will say unto me, and what I shall answer when I am reproved."

One reason people have no vision is because they don't look to the right source for vision. We try to gather ideas from listening only to others, rather than listening to God first. God will lead us to others in time. We look at what God is doing with other people who are successful, and we try to duplicate their activities and call it our vision. However, the biblical pattern of vision is that vision comes from God.

Habakkuk waited for God's answer. The text tells us that God answered and gave Habakkuk a vision—a new revelation. God allowed Habakkuk to see what God wanted. Vision is *seeing* what God wants to do in us, with us, through us, for us, *and even without us.* Vision is being able to see things as God sees them, or as God reveals them.

We need to be led by the Spirit in order to have biblical vision. Many people have ideas, but they are not necessarily biblical vision. God gives vision. A vision is different from goals and objectives. Vision is where you are headed; goals and objectives follow vision.

Vision is future-oriented. Vision is what God grants to an individual. God may allow different people to see the same thing, but vision is never the decision of a board meeting. Vision does not come from a church meeting. Vision comes from God. Vision goes beyond what we see to envisioning what can be. The apostle Paul recognized this possibility when he wrote, "Now unto him that is able to do exceeding abundantly above all that we ask or think, according to the power that worketh in us" (Eph. 3:20).

There is no question about the origin of Habakkuk's vision. God answered Habakkuk. God spoke to Habakkuk. God gave him the vision. Keep in mind that we have the Bible as our guide. What we call vision must not conflict with God's Word. God speaks to us through His Word.

## The Vision Should Be Plainly Written (2:2)

"And the LORD answered me, and said, Write the vision, and make it plain upon tables, that he may run that readeth it."

The Lord instructs Habakkuk to write down the vision so that it will be preserved. One of the problems that many would-be visionaries have is that we do not like to write things down. God instructs Habakkuk to write down what he sees. Anointed men and women throughout the ages have preserved their eyewitness accounts of God's divine deeds in human history. It began through the oral tradition of telling their stories of what God had done, and then as they were moved by the Holy Spirit they wrote it down. This is how we are blessed to have much of the Scriptures today.

If we, as the body of Christ, seek to persuade others to accept our vision as their vision, we must write it down. This is particularly true when trying to convince a congregation or an organization that what we see as the will of God is a clear direction for them. All people should be able to read it so as to share in it as those fully informed of the contents. As Habakkuk was instructed to make the vision plain, we should do the same. There's no need to write a multilevel theological construct. Keep the vision simple so anyone can understand it and allow it to speak to their hearts. Many do not have confidence in our vision because they don't understand it. Often, we try to make spiritual things dark and mysterious. But God said, "Make it plain."

God also said, "That he may run that readeth it." Now there are various ways of interpreting this clause. Some say that God is saying that the vision should be plain so that the person reading it can understand it and can intelligently communicate it with others. I personally believe that the vision should be plain, so it is easily understood—even a child can comprehend what God wants us to do. People cannot run with a vision that they do not understand. While I may not know how the Holy One is going to do what has been shown to us, I should be able to understand and comprehend the words of the vision. As we communicate it to others, it must be done in a manner that is understood by those we are communicating with.

We should not try to be so theologically deep with our interpretation of the vision that others cannot easily comprehend what is before them. God did not intend for

Habakkuk to keep the vision to himself, and neither should we. Unless God gives specific instructions to do otherwise, we should write down the vision and use our technology and resources to present it as widely and clearly as possible. We might use PowerPoint on a large screen, make posters with pictures and color that show how the vision will change our communities, or present it in an attractive and eye-catching manner for the elderly, children, men, women, people of all ages and ethnicities.

## The Vision Has a Season (2:3)

"For the vision is yet for an appointed time."

Sometimes what the Lord shows you is not immediate. If God has shown you something, it has an appointed time. The present might not be your season. It might not be your time. But the vision has a season. We cannot rush it. It comes to fruition in God's time. The phrase "appointed time" is from a Hebrew word meaning "a determined time or place without regard for the purpose." If God has given you a vision, know that it has an appointed time or a season.

I am reminded of when Mary came to Jesus at the wedding feast in Cana and told Him of the problem that there was no more wine. Jesus said that His time was not yet. It was not the time for Him to fully reveal Himself for who He was. That may have been the wish of Mary's heart, but it was not what Jesus was going to do.

Ecclesiastes 3:1 says, "To every thing there is a season, and a time to every purpose under the heaven." The vision that God has given has a season. While we may not know exactly when God will do certain things, we must trust that God has it all in control. God told Habakkuk, "For the vision is yet for an appointed time, but at the end it shall speak, and not lie" (2:3). The NIV renders it, "For the revelation awaits an appointed time; it speaks of the end and will not prove false." Although a period of time would occur before the vision is fulfilled, the vision will be fulfilled. If God has shown you something, it will come to pass in its season.

## Don't Give Up on the Vision (2:3)

"Though it tarry, wait for it; because it will surely come, it will not tarry."

Too many people become discouraged because God does not immediately perform what has been declared. God does not want Habakkuk to become discouraged because judgment on the Chaldeans is slow. God tells him that though it tarries, he should nevertheless wait for it. It will surely come. There is no doubt about it. The vision will come to pass.

The Bible has much to say about waiting on the Lord. As a matter of fact, we benefit when we wait on Him. Unfortunately, many of us can't wait, don't wait, and won't wait. We are concerned about getting our answer and deliverance now. The old saints held onto their faith in God saying, "He may not come when you want Him, but He's always on time."

The Hebrew word *qavah* means "to eagerly wait for hope." The Bible defines waiting patiently on the Lord as, "to look for with eager expectation." Usually, when the

Lord plans to bless us, it requires waiting. God uses waiting to test our obedience. For example:

- Abraham waited twenty-five years for Isaac, the child of promise
- David waited seventeen years after being anointed before becoming king of Israel
- The Jews waited forty-two generations for the Messiah

We have waited more than two thousand years for the Lord's return. Some have given up and don't believe it's true, yet countless others do believe.

If you believe your vision came from God, don't give up on your vision. Wait for its full manifestation. It will come. Impatience is a sign of immaturity. Babies want what they want at the moment they want it. Unfortunately, some have not grown beyond the baby stage. However, Isaiah 40:31 says, "But they that wait upon the LORD shall renew their strength; they shall mount up with wings as eagles; they shall run, and not be weary; and they shall walk, and not faint."

## Walk by Faith (2:4)

"Behold, his soul which is lifted up is not upright in him: but the just shall live by his faith."

Here we find the heart of God's message to Habakkuk. God gives a contrast between the proud and the just. The proud is an obvious reference to the Chaldeans. God said, "See, the enemy is puffed up; his desires are not upright" (NIV).

The Chaldeans were arrogant and proud. They depended upon themselves. That is not the way God's people are to live. Despite Habakkuk's problems with God, the Lord shows him how believers are to walk: *The just live by faith.* Although your vision may be long in coming, you are expected to live by faith. A life of faith consists of waiting on God's time to achieve God's purposes. Our job is to learn how to wait patiently, purposefully, and productively.

This statement, "The just shall live by his faith," is repeated through Scripture in Galatians 3:11, Romans 1:17, and Hebrews 10:38. It is a foundational idea for us as believers. *Faith is not only a one-time act. Faith is a way of life.*

Faith begins with being convinced that what God says is indeed true. Faith comes by hearing and hearing by the Word of God. That hearing will then govern how you live. Many say they believe what God says is true, yet their lifestyles do not reflect such a belief. So, if the vision is slow in coming, such persons easily abandon it. Those who live by faith have a lifestyle that reflects their hope and trust in God.

If we are going to be productive in the service of the Lord, we must be people of vision, lest we perish without it. God's Word instructs us what we are to do with the vision. We are to plainly write down the vision that God gives us. We should also know that the vision has a season. We should not give up on the vision as we await for the right season. As we wait, we are to have faith, and as Dr. Lawrence Neal Jones, former Dean of Howard University School of Divinity, often said, "Trust in the trustworthiness of God."

One of the things I found amazing about Ray Charles in the movie *Ray* is how he learned to function without sight. He learned how to deal with a world of darkness by seeing what others could not see. That is why God gives us vision. In a world darkened by sin, we see the light. We see not only what is, but what can be. We believe a better day is coming.

While attending a convention in Detroit, I was waiting in line at the hotel once it opened for check-in, and the line extended around the corner. I was near the back of the line when a gentleman asked me how far we had to go as we turned the corner. Unfortunately, I was in the back with him and did not know. I gave him a bit of vision that he did not appreciate. I told him, "I don't know how far we have to go once we reach the bend in the line. However, if we keep walking, more will be revealed."

Far too many people are content to stand behind and wonder how far they have to go. They miss the idea that if you keep walking by faith, God continues to reveal more and more to you. You'll be able to see what you could not see before.

In the seventh century BC, Habakkuk cried out, "O Lord, how long shall I cry, and thou wilt not hear!" (1:2). In the twentieth century, the Reverend Dr. Martin Luther King Jr., a Baptist pastor and civil rights activist, witnessed racist violence and evil in our country against God's sun-kissed children and cried out, "How long?" Like Habakkuk, Dr. King had a dream—a vision that one day there would no longer be dogs attacking black women and children peacefully demonstrating for human rights, no more black bodies hanging from trees, no more segregated schools, no more "for whites only" water fountains, and all people would have the right to vote.

On March 7, 1965, over six hundred voting rights

demonstrators—black and white, lay and clergy—marched 54 miles from Selma, Alabama, across the Edmund Pettis Bridge to Governor George Wallace's office in Montgomery demanding their right to vote as US citizens. That day became known as "Bloody Sunday" because armed police brutally attacked the peaceful demonstrators with horses, billy clubs, and tear gas.

The demonstrators crossed the bridge again on March 21 and successfully marched to the Capitol building. When they reached the state Capitol, Dr. King delivered a speech to inspire the marchers. He said,

> I know you are asking today, "How long will it take?" Somebody's asking, "How long will prejudice blind the visions of men, darken their understanding, and drive bright-eyed wisdom from her sacred throne?" . . .
>
> I come to say to you this afternoon, however difficult the moment, however frustrating the hour, it will not be long, because "truth crushed to earth will rise again."
>
> How long? Not long, because "no lie can live forever."
>
> How long? Not long, because "you shall reap what you sow."
>
> How long? Not long:
> Truth forever on the scaffold,
> Wrong forever on the throne,
> Yet that scaffold sways the future,
> And, behind the dim unknown,
> Standeth God within the shadow.[2]

2. Dr. Martin Luther King Jr., "Our God is Marching On!" (speech, Montgomery, AL, March 25, 1965), Stanford, The Martin Luther King, Jr. Research and Education Institute, https://kinginstitute.stanford.edu/our-god-marching.

When God answered Habakkuk in a vision, his complaints and questions were silenced as he stood with renewed faith in God. Habakkuk wrote an affirmation of faith for himself, and the righteous remnant of Judah:

> Although the fig tree shall not blossom, neither shall fruit be in the vines; the labour of the olive shall fail, and the fields shall yield no meat; the flock shall be cut off from the fold, and there shall be no herd in the stalls: Yet I will rejoice in the Lord, I will joy in the God of my salvation. The Lord God is my strength, and he will make my feet like hinds' feet, and he will make me to walk upon mine high places. (Hab. 3:17–19)

# CHAPTER 8

# HIS WORD WORKS

*Expository Preaching from an Old Testament
Prophetic Book, Largely Narrative*

## JONAH 3
### CHARLIE E. DATES

This sermon was first preached as the third of a four-part series through the book of Jonah. The aim of the series was to inspire the congregation toward an active, not reluctant, gospel engagement with our community in Chicago. This particular message focuses on the sufficiency and authority of the Scripture in our evangelism. It is my conviction that the witness of the church is that the Word of God works—with or without our full cooperation. In a world where people are trying all manner of would-be alternatives; where even Christians are tempted to view the influence of Scripture as a prize of yesteryear, the encouragement of Jonah 3 is needed today. Theologically, it explores the omnibenevolent character of God by illustrating His concern for people, all people, especially those encapsulated by a wicked society. The cities of our day need churches that actively evangelize. As we can see in the repentance of Nineveh in Jonah 3, the social is renewed by the theological. It is the good news of God, the invitation of repentance that radically changed Nineveh, even if it was scornfully proclaimed by the prophet who keynoted the revival. This sermon was delivered in the morning services at Progressive Baptist Church in Chicago during the summer of 2018.

## INTRODUCTION

The proposition of Jonah 3 is clear: *Human rebellion does not defeat Divine sovereignty.*

History is the evidence of that truth. From Diocletian to Thomas Jefferson to the slave Bible, the work of emperors and civic leaders have been unable to stop God's Word. You can see it in the Great Persecution undertaken by Diocletian and the events following. That Roman emperor ordered the burning of Christian Scriptures and decreed death for any person who would not sacrifice to the gods. He imprisoned the preachers, murdered Christians, set their villages to flames. In fact, he took their Scriptures and burned them to ashes.

Not even ten years later, young Constantine came to power. Whatever you make of his brand of faith, he legalized Christianity in Rome and prompted the spread of Christianity. The church took off again, because not even world rulers can stop the Book.

You can see it in Voltaire, that notorious French philosopher. In 1778, he boasted that within one hundred years the Bible would be no more. Later, Voltaire died, and in 1836 the President of the Evangelical Society made a home in Les Delices, Voltaire's old house. That house became a repository for Bibles and tracts, because not even world-class philosophers can restrain the power of God's Word.[1]

And what shall we say about those enslaved Africans, fresh to the shores of the colonies in America? The Society for the Conversion of Negro Slaves, a name laughable in itself, produced a "missionary book" known as The Slave Bible. Their efforts at conversion were but a thin veil to enslave the minds and souls of African people. These "missionary books" were redacted Bibles. Passages about freedom, liberation, and the love of God for all humanity were completely removed. They went so far as to erase the entire book of Exodus from the Bible. Yet those slave preachers, those men and women made in the image of God from the shores of Africa, read through those redacted Bibles, kept turning the pages, kept praying until they discovered that ours is a God of liberation. The very book that was meant to imprison them became the tool of their greatest freedom. The Bible, and their particular understanding of it, liberated their theology and gave birth to America's black church because not even economic superpowers can stop the Book.

We have many contemporary pundits declaring the death of the Word of God. But those who have placed the Bible in the casket of irrelevance, and lowered it down into the ground of disregard, have only come to discover that the Bible survives its undertakers.

---

1. The British and Foreign Bible Society, *The Missionary Register*, vol. 24 (London: L&G Seeley, 1836), 352, https://books.google.com.au/books?id=IH0oAA AAYAAJ&pg=PA352&redir_esc=y#v=onepage&q=voltaire&f=false.

God's word is unrelenting.
His truth is everlasting.
His commands are enduring.
His gospel is indestructible.
His judgments are indisputable.
His corrections are timeless.
This Book is fresher than tomorrow's newspaper.
It is more definite than the constitution.
It is the backbone of science.
It is the highest aim of philosophy.
It is the inspiration of poetry.

It will clarify your call to ministry.
It will transform your life.
It will fight your temptations.
It will light your path.
It will build your faith.
It will feed your soul.

Time cannot age this book and ages do not time it.
You have read many books, but this is the only book
that has read you.

Herod couldn't stop it.
Diocletian couldn't destroy it.
Nero couldn't tame it.
Hitler couldn't change it.
Jefferson couldn't erase it.
Jordan Peterson can't reduce it.

Saul couldn't kill it.
Moses tried to record it.
Jeremiah couldn't drop it.
Hosea couldn't divorce it.
And, in our text, Jonah couldn't run from it.

It is the timeless, indestructible, self-sustaining, eternal Word of God.

Perhaps we get no greater illustration of the unrelenting, unstoppable nature of the Word of God than in the life of Jonah, the wayward Hebrew prophet. His story teaches us something about the nature and jurisdiction of the Word of God: *When you run from it, it will run into you.*

How did Jonah get to Nineveh? That is a question that the narrative of this eighth-century prophet wants us to ask. There was no pulpit search committee in Nineveh, no mission's board to recommend a revivalist for the pending reformation of Assyria. From all historical-cultural clues, there was no volunteer prophet willing to reach beyond his own nationalist, ethnocentric, and culturally narrow conception of the mercy of God.

So how did Jonah get to Nineveh? One can hardly blame Jonah for not wanting to "Go" to the palace of paganism. After all, Nineveh is synonymous with terrorism.

It would be hard to exaggerate the wickedness that characterized this capital city of the Assyrian Empire. In war, the Ninevites played the game of psychological warfare. They were a kind of experimental terrorist society. Deficient in natural resources and short on military supply, when Nineveh came to fight, they did not come to fight long. They would force their conquered enemies to impale one another on poles, dismember and disfigure their fallen comrades.

The interest was public relations. Nineveh wanted word spread about their method of warfare so that subsequent opponents would simply accept a suzerain treaty in lieu of waging war. Some scholars suggest that the Romans first heard of crucifixion from the Assyrians. These were evil men. Who could blame Jonah for not wanting to go to Nineveh?

Who could blame you for not wanting to preach to a culture, growing increasingly hostile to the gospel? Who among us is eager to face the gallows of public opinion? What Christian is enthused about the certain rejection of family or friends for affirming what the world considers to be the archaic, outmoded message of Scripture?

But we learn from Jonah how God's Word works. God's Word works in spite of us, not because of us. It works through us, not by reason of us. It works with us, not by the help of us.

I want to raise from this passage, this quick series of insights about how God's Word works to safeguard His purposes and secure His prophets.

## His Word Works with Us, Not by the Help of Us

### It's God's Prerogative

The first commendation at the curtain raising of our text is a word about the authority and jurisdiction of the Word of God. Jonah 3:1 reminds us that salvation comes by the prerogative of God, not the initiative of men. This is how Jonah gets to Nineveh. Watch it closely: The Word of the Lord came to Jonah.

Remember now that we don't come to the word of the Lord. The sequence of events is always that the word of the Lord comes to us. This is a not-so-subtle rebuttal against every self-appointed prophet, every government-chosen preacher, and every tribe-delegated culture warrior. God, through His own initiative, calls preachers, appoints missionaries, and raises leaders. It is the word of God that arrests Jonah, convicts Jonah, pursues Jonah, and then employs Jonah. It is God's word that overrules Jonah's rebellion.

There may be a measure of comic relief in Jonah's attempt to flee from the presence of God, but here is likely a more striking caution for the emerging Christian leader. At a time where temptation toward celebrity almost out-motivates the mandate for ministry, when a calling is treated as a career, and when the lure of self-adoration can overpower a basic love for God, Jonah's story warns us: Don't go if God hasn't called you.

I remember applying for a grant from a popular theological education fund. In the course of a few conversations, I was asked to endorse a particular program. When telling me about the program, the representative said, "It's not so much that you feel this inward tug to preach, but that the church spots you. Perhaps a Sunday school teacher says you have the gift, and the church makes you a preacher. The congregation calls you to preach."

I respectfully declined because after years in ministry, I've come to learn that whoever calls you has to keep you.

And what happens when the church that called you does not want you to preach anymore?

No, the congregation does not call. God calls. That is the biblical model. The word of the Lord arrested Jonah and sent him to Nineveh. His word has to arrest your heart and issue you no other alternative.

None of us preach because the church called us. You think I preach because a church called me? You think I'm standing here because they gave me an opportunity? We don't preach because people are nice, kind, or have selected us. We preach because God compels us. We go because His word sends us. We preach because He will let us do nothing else. We preach because, like Jeremiah said, His word is like fire shut up in our bones (Jer. 20:9). That's the kind of preachers our nation needs!

### A Second Chance

Now read Jonah 3:1 in contradistinction to 1:1. The opening constructions of chapters 1 and 3 are meant to signal to the careful reader overwhelming similarity. They read almost exactly the same. It is a clue not only to the fact that chapter 3 is a turning point in the overarching literary narrative of Jonah, but that chapter 3 is a second chance for the wayward prophet himself. The glaring difference is the phrase "a second time" (3:1). It's as if the narrator wants you and me to feel the peculiarity of this moment. God's word came to Jonah—wait for it—"a *second* time."

Do you know how hard it is to get a second time in life? Right now, there are approximately 2,500 children in the United States sentenced to juvenile life without parole. That's 2,500 children as young as 13 who will never get another chance at life outside of prison. Our society is so constituted that there are some offenses for which you never get a second time.

After all that Jonah had been through, chapter 3 is a shocking declaration. He should have died in his disobedience. He should have lost his ordination by reason of his open rebellion. He should have never been used of God again because of His outright insubordination. But do you know what God likes to do with people who measure their defiance against God's kindness? *He arranges the circumstances so that grace is not an abstract theological proposition but a concrete lived experience.*

The Word of God is a book of second chances. It is a clue into how God deals with His beloved:

- Moses got another chance after he threw those stone tablets in Exodus 32
- God gave David a second chance after adultery and murder in 2 Samuel 11
- God gave Hezekiah another shot when he turned his face to the wall in prayer
- Isaiah found another chance as a prolific prophet although he was a man of unclean lips
- Gomer received more than a second chance after her repeated trysts outside of her marriage
- And think of Peter, Paul, and Mark, whose rebellion was no match for God's grace

His Word works with us. When we would rebel, we discover the strength of His work requires not our assistance. It is the Word of God that turns us from our willful rebellion! Jonah 3 is the proclamation that God comes after us; that He sends His Word as the hound dog of mercy.

## His Word Works in Spite of Us, Not Because of Us

*The Purposes of God, Not the Plans of Men*

God works in spite of Jonah to accomplish the outreach to Nineveh. God used the failure of Jonah as an illustration of mercy to Nineveh. All Jonah had to do was show up and preach. His very existence was the evidence that mercy works. This is a great city to God. God loves these people.

Nineveh is strikingly called "great in relationship to God." This phrase in the Hebrew language may be taken several ways. Nineveh may be great *before* God (4:11) or great *to* God. One has to wonder what the emphasis of a great city means to God. We live in a great city. Beyond the vast skyline, and the prodigious sky scrapper buildings, Chicagoland has a population of more than eight million people. In our neighborhood alone is more than one hundred thousand, some of whom won't know the joy of a satisfied life in God. Even with our collection of churches, and our cohort of excellent gospel preachers, Chicago might be a lot like Nineveh: godless, violent, and politically complicit. And yet, like Nineveh, God cares about Chicago. He cares for every city where people reside.

That's especially good news for us who live in large metropolitan cities. He cares for Cairo with its nearly twenty-four million people surrounding the ancient architecture of the old pyramids. He cares for Instanbul with its fifteen million people following a false substitute for the one true God. Here is the truth of our passage: God loves them just as much as if there's only one of them to love.

Dr. Joel Gregory says it this way, "An infinite God cares infinitely for an infinite number of people."[2] That is fascinating. Even the above-average pastor has a hard time loving just a few people.

I know many people whose faith is so narrow, parochial, and nearsighted that they believe like Jonah that God cares for only one nation (our nation) and one nationality (our nationality)—America first and build walls to keep it that way! It's difficult for us to see that God wants to wrap His arms around the whole world, including our national and religious enemies. In New Jersey, a man is neglecting his family, in Scotland a child is being abused, and in India a family is being devastated by poverty—and yet an infinite God cares infinitely that each of those people hear His voice and be redeemed.

## Mercy on Display

Embedded in Jonah's message of judgment is what Deitrich Bonhoeffer called the germ of grace. Look at the distinction between this verse construction and that of chapter 1. In chapter 1, God told Jonah to go and cry *against* Nineveh. In chapter 3, God tells Jonah to go and proclaim *to* Nineveh the proclamation that He would tell him.

*All preaching of the gospel points to the mercy of God.* This slight and subtle shift of the preposition is a window

---

2. A term Joel Gregory used in a personal correspondence with me.

into the unrelenting mercy of God. That Jonah is to preach to them instead of against them is as significant an unveiling of God's purposes that either Nineveh or Jonah could have imagined.

### Proclaim the Proclamation

Notice how the text implies the source of the strength of our preaching and evangelism. The efficacy of our preaching is tethered not to the eloquence of the preacher, but to the word we preach. Jonah's message is to be straight from God's mouth. Here is the real power in preaching. The proclamation from the prophet does not originate in the mind of the prophet. He is not the source of its content or the motivation of his own feelings. Authentic preaching is God's word in the prophet's mouth. The authority of preaching is in the author of the message, not the personality of the messenger. It is the word that works, not the preacher who makes the word work.

I once sat with a friend who shared a fascinating story about his church's new pastor. As an aspiring pastor, his words grabbed me with a strange peculiarity. He loved their new pastor, and felt somewhat relieved that their old pastor had moved on. Wanting to know how I could avoid whatever pitfalls he would share, I probed further. My friend told me that the old pastor was always telling the church what was wrong with them, how they were displeasing God. He said the old pastor said it with a kind of joy or glee. I get that now, having served in ministry for a while. There are times when people unnerve you and despite the caring heart the preacher should possess, there is a subtle desire that God prove His righteousness by exacting punishment on His rebellious people. That's terrible, but true. The tragic part of my friend's revelation is that their pastor actually preached about their judgment with a kind of enthusiasm. Their new pastor was no less relenting, but far more brokenhearted about it. He told me that the new pastor wept with the people, and pleaded with them to turn from their rebellion and turn to God.

Feel the pitiful, graceless preaching of Jonah. In the Hebrew tongue, his sermon is only five words long. A sermon doesn't have to be eternal to be everlasting! Yet forty days! Why not, "Yet this weekend?" Why not, "Yet tonight?" *It is a sermon of judgment, but in it is the bacteria of grace.* The word always includes grace. Jonah's is a sad sermon, but it still works because it's not the preacher that works, but the word God gives to the preacher that works.

## His Word Works through Us, Not by Reason of Us

There's something that happens when we preach. I'll say it again. There's something that happens when we preach. God takes His word and does the unpredictable. You can never fully tell just what God might do when His word is preached. He quickens the hearts of the hearers. He changes the minds of the obstinate. He softens the grip of the hoarder. He renews the lifeless spirit. Paul said it like this: "faith comes from hearing the message, and the message is heard through the word about Christ" (Rom. 10:17 NIV).

You don't believe me? Look at what happens to the wicked city of Nineveh. Look at Sennacherib's capital empire. See what happens. From the youngest to the oldest, from the weakest to the most powerful, from the dogs to the cats, from the neighborhoods to City Hall—all of Nineveh repented. God can save anybody.

This is unpredictable. Excavators tell us that Nineveh was eventually destroyed, but what they cannot tell us is how this repentance altered the course of human history. History is our witness that God's Word brings about unpredictable results. One seed of God's Word changes the course of human history:

- It took only one seed of His Word to touch the heart of Joan Kroc as a girl, and the Salvation Army benefitted all the more
- It took one seed of His Word to touch the heart of Jeremy Lanphier, and the businessman's revival took the East Coast by storm
- It took one seed of His Word to grab the mind and ministry of Gardner Calvin Taylor, and the genius of black preaching reached a fever pitch of homiletical poetry
- It took one seed of His Word to make Clay Evans stand against Mayor Richard J. Daley, and a great church on the South Side ushered a new era to Chicago

We keep preaching His word even though we cannot reason what good it will do.

# PART 3

---

# Biblical Exposition
# of the New Testament

# WHO IS THIS MAN?

### *Expository Preaching from the Gospels and Acts*

---

## MARK 5
### ROMELL WILLIAMS

---

This sermon was preached at a Sunday morning worship service at Lilydale M. B. Church in the spring of 2019. It was part of an expositional series on the Gospel of Mark. I am able to preach the full chapter in one message because there are three ministories bound within one broad geographic region (see 5:1 with 6:1). This chapter continues Mark's initial thesis that Jesus is the Son of God. Interestingly, Mark uses a question about Jesus' identity posed at the end of chapter 4 to now carry along and cement his argument. The three stories that follow are all structured with a perfect narrative plot arc. They each have setting, conflict, climax, resolution, and a new setting embedded within their literary arrangements. When we process each one individually the climax of all three stories is an encounter with Jesus, which addresses and supernaturally removes each person's problem. He is the main character of the chapter, and His identity is what Mark is spotlighting in these stories and with these supporting characters. Unfortunately, throughout church history we have given center stage to the possessed, the infirmed, and the deceased, not to Jesus. This has caused us to miss the author's aim and to divide these stories, which were designed to be told together.

The major interpretive issue of this passage seeks to resolve why a chapter with this much power on display closes with a prohibition and not a proclamation: "He gave strict orders not to let anyone know about this, and told them to give her something to eat" (5:43). Jesus tells the demoniac to go home, and He sends the formerly hemorrhaging woman away in peace (5:19, 34). Why does He hide the miracle of raising the girl from the dead? The oddity of this dissimilarity and its great asynchronous presence in comparison to the two previous commissions of grace act like a neon sign for the reader that says, "Park here for a minute, think and pray!"

Once one has identified the theological truth to which that literary abnormality was pointing, the rest of the passage spreads open like a day lily on an early spring morning. The remaining challenge was to help my church reason to the conclusions that the Gospel writer wants us to draw.

## INTRODUCTION

Periodically, reality TV strikes entertainment gold. This is exactly what they've done with the multiple Emmy award-winning show *Undercover Boss*. This ingenious television series chronicles the descent of some high-level executive or entrepreneur into the rank and file of their own company. These men and women are disguised and then inserted into the company culture at an entry-level.

The show revolves around their experiences while undercover. The lessons they learn from their employees are both interesting and profound. The first-hand opportunities to see, hear, and process the companies they captain are invaluable. Most importantly, the relationships they establish with other members of their human resources team, without the issues of seniority or management, allow for honest, heartfelt, and hilarious exchanges that supply the unique context that makes this show so popular.

After several weeks of working undercover, the boss returns to his or her proper position. The corporate office then sends for, and schedules, a series reveal meetings. In these surprising instances, the individuals who have rubbed elbows with their bosses unknowingly are made aware of their employer's true identity. This unique way of concluding each episode and each journey yields a variety of interesting fruit. These shows resolve with promotions, improvements, bonuses, and sometimes even terminations, based on the information that has been gleaned and processed by the boss while undercover.[1]

This ingenious reality TV concept is really not an original idea. For you see in Christ, God Himself became the undercover boss, as it were. He took upon Himself human nature so He could both inspect and correct creation from within. His purpose wasn't comprehension, promotion, or termination. God in Christ came to our world for the high purpose of redemption.

When we consider Mark 5, we discover that unlike the show, Jesus did not summon people to corporate headquarters to reveal His true identity. No, friends. He simply

---

1. "*Undercover Boss*," Wikipedia, last edited October 3, 2019, https://en.wikipedia.org/wiki/Undercover_Boss.

used the extreme circumstances that were beyond people's control to disclose and demonstrate His identity as the one who has complete control.

Today, in the time that we share, I want to ask you three questions, tell you three stories, make three applications, and then arrive at one conclusion.

For far too long we have divorced, separated, and compartmentalized what God and Mark intended to be joined together. Countless messages have been preached in city temples and country churches about this man, this woman, and this little girl. But their stories, although complete on their own, are designed to transmit the same truth from three different perspectives. These stories aren't about these people. No, they are intended to announce that amidst our hopelessness, there exists One in whom we can all place our hopes.

## Who Is This Man with Authority over Demons?

In this first story, Jesus has just crossed over. The Lord has travelled from Galilee to Gadara, and He and His disciples are met by a strange individual welcome party. Out from the tombs, a man comes running and then he kneels at the feet of Jesus. This mysterious sight is both disturbing and confusing. Out from the graveyard, he comes covered in filth, blood, sweat, and scabs, but he drops to his knees in front of Jesus, calling Him the "Son of the Most High God!"

Mark provides us with the inside scoop. We are informed that this man had an unclean spirit. He has moved out of town and into the cemetery. The citizens have repeatedly attempted to restrain him, but to no avail. The supernatural presence in his person has multiplied his physical strength. He breaks chains and handcuffs and anything else they try to use to restrict him.

Nobody can calm him down. This guy is all the way gone. He lives among the dead, and they can hear him screaming both night and day, as that which is within him keeps trying to destroy him from the inside out. He appears by all accounts to be a maniac, but in truth he's something worse. He hasn't lost his mind. No, friends. His mind has been taken over. This hopeless man is demon possessed!

When we take a closer look, what appears to be humility is actually strategy. The force that controls this man is hoping to outwit Jesus in false surrender and be left to continue its reign of terror inside this man who has been abandoned by everyone else. The text is clear that Jesus offers continuous commands for the demon to come out of the human. Then Jesus asked a single question that called this evil into accountability: "What is your name?" (v. 9).

Finally, it happens: The voice that must have sounded like a symphony announces the multitude of evil that is now fighting to hold on at Jesus' command to get out. "My name is Legion, for we are many!"

Oh no! Legion! Friends, a legion was the military designation for six thousand Roman soldiers. This doesn't mean that this exact number of evil spirits inhabited this single person. It does mean that there was far more than just one, one hundred, or even one thousand demons who had taken hold of this poor guy. Dr. Ralph West calls him "a human haunted house." This uncounted army of fallen angels had death-marched across the landscape of this man's soul. But their time was up, and they knew it the moment Jesus got off the boat.

So after giving a name and suggesting a number, they plea for permission. Knowing they have to leave the man, they beg for a divine permission slip to possess or take control of a nearby herd of pigs. Jesus grants this request for the immediate release of the man, to further prove His power over these demons, and to let us see the final design of demonic activity. Into the swine legion goes, not to live in comfort, but to die in control. After taking the two thousand pigs as their new host, these demons immediately drive the swine over the cliff to their deaths. This is because Satan's goal is destruction, not just possession.

Then the unthinkable happens. Those tending the pigs alerted the citizens to this strange set of events. So everyone walks out to the seaside to take a look. What they find is so shocking that something had to be done—immediately. This same man who was living in the tombs, cutting himself with stones, screaming day and night, is now calmly seated at the feet of Jesus. He is clothed and in his right mind. He knows his name, and his history because Jesus has now edited his hopeless story. Sadly, the people of the region are unable to comprehend that they have witnessed a miracle, and ignorantly request that Jesus leave the community because they don't know what to do with Him.

Jesus prepares to depart, and the delivered man requests to enter the discipleship training program. But his application is denied. This guy was delivered to be a witness. Jesus tells him to stay where he was once hopeless in order to announce to his family, friends, and neighbors where he had found hope! "Go . . . and tell them how much the Lord has done for you, and how he has had mercy on you!" It's as if He said, "Stay here, son, so you can announce My identity and proclaim My activity."

My name used to be Legion! If you are aware of a time when the devil had control of you and Jesus set you free, Legion's story is your story. If the enemy ever tried to use you to destroy yourself, his story is your story. If you have felt the presence and power of evil at work in your life, but God intervened on your behalf, his story is your story. Now that Jesus has made a difference, your responsibility is the same as this man! Go and tell everyone you can that Jesus saved you from Satan and even from yourself.

## Who Is This Man with Authority over Disease?

In this second story, Jesus has crossed the Sea of Galilee again. While He is virtually unknown in the Decapolis, His fame is widespread in this area. This time, a crowd meets Him at the seaside. This enthusiastic crowd has within it a man and a woman who desperately need Jesus' help. The man's name is Jairus, and he is a synagogue ruler with a sick daughter at the point of death. He finds Jesus, falls at His feet, and begs that Jesus come and heal his daughter. Graciously, the Lord consents to follow Jairus home. As they begin their trek, another person consumed by hopelessness sees her chance. She is a woman and she has an issue.

For the second time, Mark now offers the inside scoop. This sick lady has been suffering for a long time. Twelve years to be exact. She has been bleeding—menstruating, not for seven days, seven weeks, or seven months. No, this hurting woman has been losing her life-source constantly for twelve years! She is ceremonially unclean, according to Jewish standards. Then to add insult to injury, we are told that she's gone to countless doctors and tried countless remedies, but her situation is not getting better. In fact, it's growing worse.

Jesus is her last hope, and she doesn't even ask for His help. She's in such bad shape that we aren't even given her name because she's become known by her issue. The extreme nature of her circumstances has purified her faith. So she presses her way through this massive crowd while repeating herself to herself: "If Jesus is who they say He is, and if He can do what I heard He can do, I don't need an audience. I just need to make contact. If I can just touch Him, I'll be made well."

Guess what happened? She gets to Jesus and stretches out her hand, touches His clothes, and receives her healing. There was faith, a touch, and then a miracle. He is the contact point between heaven's power and humanity's problems. So when she touched His cloak, she was healed by Him. Mark says, "Immediately her bleeding stopped and she felt in her body that she was freed from her suffering" (NIV).

But wait one minute. She won't get away easily. No healings are happening today without Jesus signing off on them. He felt power leave Him and go to her. So the Lord, fully aware of what's transpired and determined to make her testimony a matter of public records, asks, "Who touched my clothes?" (v. 30). His disciples try to reason with the master. "With all these people in this crowd, now you want to know who touched Your clothes?"

Jesus stops, the crowd halts, Jairus cringes, but the healed woman identifies herself. She's afraid, and she's shaking, but now she's at the feet of Jesus, telling Him her whole story. Perhaps she said, "Lord, I've been sick for a very long time. I have tried everything to get well, but nothing has worked. As the years have passed, my condition has gotten progressively worse. I was at the point of giving up until I heard about You. They said You heal sick people. I know I'm not supposed to be in public like this, but I had to at least touch You to see if it would work. Lord, I did, and my sickness is over, my pain has stopped, and my issue has been resolved."

Now, at the full disclosure of her testimony to the waiting masses, Jesus puts His stamp of verification on her miracle. "Daughter, your faith has healed you. Go in peace and be freed from your suffering" (NIV). This statement from the Lord addresses both her physical and spiritual transformation as a result of her faith in Christ. She was completely healed and completely saved because in her hopeless circumstance she found Jesus to be her only hope.

*He fixed my issue!* If you've been sick and God made you well, her story is your story. If you've had an issue that no one but Jesus could help you resolve, her story is your story. If you're only alive today because you made contact with Him one day, her story is your story. Go public with your testimony that when sickness and suffering are too hard for man's help, they are just right for God's power.

## Who Is This Man
## with Authority over Death?

What appears to be a delay is actually a necessary detour. Jairus needed to get off the fringes and move into complete hopelessness before his candidacy for a miracle could be confirmed. In the commotion and hold up, his terminally ill little girl died. What could be worse than that? You got to Jesus in time. He consented to follow you home. But this woman holds Him up, and now you get word from the house that it's too late. Your daughter is no longer sick; now she's dead. What will Jairus do? Well, Jesus tells him, "Don't be afraid; just believe." (v. 36). In other words, "It's not too late. Just keep walking with Me!

I believe that in this moment the only thing that kept Jairus walking was this woman's testimony. Perhaps he thought to himself, *If Jesus could heal her twelve-year condition, He can also handle the death of my twelve-year-old daughter. If her faith made her well and now He's telling me to keep believing, that's exactly what I'll do.*

Jairus obeys and continues to go home. Jesus sounds crazy because the nurses are still in the room finalizing the little girl's death certificate. The diastolic and systolic heart readings have ceased. She is not breathing or responding to stimuli. The IV is unplugged, and the white sheet has been pulled over her head. But the Master walks in and clears her hospice room because He intends to turn it into her resurrection site.

Jesus clears the room of all who did not have faith. He takes with Him to witness this miracle only His inner circle of Peter, James, and John. The Master walks over to this dead child and commands her to get up. Sooner than right now and quicker than at once, Jairus's daughter who was dead is now alive again!

*"Arise!" is what He commands the dead to do!* If anything has died in your life, Jairus and his little girl's story is your story. If you've done all you could and things still went awry until Jesus showed up, their story is your story. If you've ever been surrounded by doubt, but Jesus came through in a crunch, their story is your story.

Why does a chapter with this much power on display close with a prohibition and not a proclamation? Delivering the demonic is dangerous; healing the sick is not safe; *but raising the dead will get you killed.* In fact, when we trace the Scriptures, this is the very straw that broke the camel's back in John 11 and caused Jesus' adversaries to pursue the death penalty.

*But it's not Jesus' time to die yet.* He will go to the cross. He will be our sacrifice for sin. He will endure God's judgment on our behalf. It's not His time yet. So the text says, "And he strictly charged them that no one should know this, and told them to give her something to eat" (ESV).

Mark 5 is Mark's attempt to answer the disciples' question from Mark 4:41 (ESV): "And they were filled with great fear and said to one another, 'Who then is this, that even the wind and the sea obey him?'" Who is this Man? *He's Jesus Christ, the Son of God!*

In this passage, we observe every major category of personhood (or humanity) with a *man,* a *woman,* and a *child.* Then we are given every major category of problems with *spiritual, physical,* and *time-sensitive* issues (or hopelessness) being addressed. So here is the conclusion of which Mark is in pursuit: *Humanity plus hopelessness should lead us to the reality of who Jesus is when He intervenes as only God can.* Because He is the Son of God, no matter who you are, or what you are dealing with, an encounter with Jesus can change your life!

Your name does not matter. Your circumstances do not matter. If you have an encounter with Jesus, because He's *God* He can change anything and everything. That's the point of Mark 5: A man overrun with demons meets Jesus and gets delivered; a woman overburdened with sickness meets Jesus and her issue gets resolved; a child who has been overcome by death meets Jesus and receives new life. Jesus can make the difference for you, in you, and with you because He is God.

## Close

What a wonderful change in my life has been wrought
    Since Jesus came into my heart!
I have light in my soul for which long I had sought,
    Since Jesus came into my heart!
    Since Jesus came into my heart!
    Since Jesus came into my heart!
Floods of joy o'er my soul like the sea billows roll,
    Since Jesus came into my heart!
I have ceased from my wand'ring and going astray,
    Since Jesus came into my heart!
And my sins which were many are all washed away,
    Since Jesus came into my heart!
I'm possessed of a hope that is steadfast and sure,
    Since Jesus came into my heart!

And no dark clouds of doubt now my pathway obscure,
    Since Jesus came into my heart!
There's a light in the valley of death now for me,
    Since Jesus came into my heart!
And the gates of the City beyond I can see,
    Since Jesus came into my heart!
I shall go there to dwell in that City I know,
    Since Jesus came into my heart!
And I'm happy, so happy as onward I go,
    Since Jesus came into my heart![2]

## CONCLUSION

This message was both a challenge and a joy to share. The clear challenge revolves around how we are conditioned to read only portions of Scripture or dissected stories, not full chapters. As, I prepared to communicate, I had to make a decision about whether I would read all these verses, or simply spotlight some to get us moving into the moments of proclamation. I chose to read the sections that announced each problem in the text, and the sections where the troubled individuals collided with Jesus. This served its purpose, but I also challenged the congregation to read the full chapter in private before the day was over.

The joy of preaching this chapter was lifting up Jesus as Mark originally intended, and watching the parishioners connect as the Holy Spirit turned on the lights for them through the message. Again, many times when we handle the Scripture, the forest is missed because we are staring at some detail on a tree. Bringing

2. Rufus Henry McDaniel, "What a Wonderful Change in My Life Has Been Wrought" (1914).

the larger picture into focus and moving the emphasis from people and their problems to Jesus as the solution was paramount to this sermon's effectiveness. I worked deliberately after modernizing the retelling of each story to the listeners, and show them how Jesus can or has done these exact things in their own lives. Our preaching must cross the bridge. It cannot leave Jesus in antiquity as some historical fixer, because each week the audience has their own set of problems. Christ is the remedy then and now, because He's God and that won't ever change.

# CHAPTER 10

# HAVE YOU GOT GOOD RELIGION?

*Expository Preaching from a New Testament Epistle*

## JAMES 1:26–27

### PAUL FELIX

In preaching the book of James sequentially and expositionally, I inevitably landed at 1:19–27. Some of these verses were not familiar to the intended audience, but surely verse 22 was. It is rare for a Christian to declare unfamiliarity with the command of James to be doers of the Word.

The first challenge facing an expositor of this passage is whether to preach it as one sermon or as three (1:19–21; 1:22–25; 1:26–27). The advantage of preaching it as one sermon is that it maintains the unity of the paragraph. The listeners are convinced that the three sections are united in thought. The benefit of preaching it as three sermons is that it allows the expositor more time to drive home the weightiness of what James has written. It is easy to miss out on some of the details that are presented in these verses if they are treated in one sermon. The expositor needs to slow down and impress upon his hearers the proper interpretation of 1:19–21. Verses 19–20 are proverbial statements related to God's

Word. The hearers might be surprised that they are to be quick to hear God's Word, slow to speak God's Word, and slow to become angry with God's Word. They normally think of these statements as related to the subject of our speech.[1]

A separate sermon on 1:22–25 allows the familiar words of 1:22 and what follows to impact the audience. What is the miscalculation being made when a person is a hearer of the Word only? How does the illustration of a man looking into a mirror support the foolishness of being a hearer of the Word and not a doer (1:23–24)? What is meant by the perfect law of liberty in 1:25a? Time needs to be taken to point out the steps involved in being the blessed person of 1:25b.

Although 1:26–27 might seem like a small passage for an expositional sermon, it is not. The impact of 1:22–25 is so powerful that the two verses that follow can be viewed as an afterthought. Yet, these verses are the apex of James's argument that the heart of genuine spirituality is obedience to God's Word. These words must be seriously considered by the expositor and thus should be stressed to the intended audience of the sermon.

Convinced that James 1:26–27 is to be preached as a separate sermon, the expositor must get down to the task of exegesis. The first step is lexical exegesis. There are a variety of lexical meanings that must be addressed: (1) What is the meaning of the term "religion" since it is often proclaimed that Christianity is not a religion but a relationship? (2) Does the hypothetical man

---

1. This view is developed from the context of 1:19–21. James 1:18 speaks of the new birth by "the word of truth." James 1:21 is an exhortation to "receive the word implanted" (NASB). In the well-known James 1:22, the readers are commanded to become doers of the Word. The emphasis before and after 1:19–21 is the Word. The scholarly article that influenced my interpretation is C. John Collins, "Coherence in James 1:19-27," *Journal of Translation and Textlinguistics* 10 (1998): 80–87.

in verse 26 "think" he is religious (NASB, ESV, NIV) or does he "seem" to be religious (KJV)? (3) What is meant by bridling the tongue? (4) What does it mean that a person's religion is "vain" (KJV)? (5) What's the distinction between "religious" and "religion"? (6) How are the terms "pure" and "undefiled" to be defined (NASB, ESV, KJV)? (7) What does it mean to "visit" orphans and widows in their distress (NASB, ESV, KJV)? (8) What is the meaning of "world"? These are some of the lexical issues that must be resolved in tackling the crucial task of exegesis.

Exegesis is more than determining the meaning of nonroutine terms. A second step in the exegetical process is syntactical exegesis. Attention must be given to dealing with the significance of parts of speech, the relationship between words, the use of tenses, the function of words, the structure of the words, and so on. Syntactical exegesis is necessary when it comes to these two verses. Some questions to answer are: (1) Why is verse 26 introduce with an "if" statement (NASB, ESV, KJV)? (2) What is the function of the participle that is translated "bridle" (NASB, ESV)? (3) How is the strong adversative "but" being used in verse 26 (NASB, ESV, KJV)? (4) What is the function of the participle that is translated "deceives" (NASB, ESV)? (5) Is there any significance to the fact that technically there is no verb supplied in the phrase "this peron's religion is worthless" (ESV), even though translators have supplied one? (6) How is the preposition functioning that is translated "in the sight of" (NASB), especially since other translations render it "before" (ESV) or even ignore it (NIV)? (7) What is the role of the two infinitives "to visit" (NASB, ESV, KJV) and "to keep"? (8) Additionally, what is the best structure for these two verses?

A third element in the exegetical procedure is identifying and resolving problems. Some of these issues have already been mentioned in relation to the previous discussion of lexical exegesis and syntactical exegesis.

Exegesis is the basis of exposition. The expositor does not preach his exegesis. Neither does he incorporate all that he has gleaned from the exegetical process into the sermon. Rather, exegesis must shape and craft the sermon that is to be proclaimed. In other words, there are homiletical concerns that must be considered if 1:26–27 is to be preached faithfully. What is the key idea of these two verses? What is it that you as an expositor are trying to persuade your audience of from this text? You are preaching primarily to an African American audience. Will you include a song in your sermon that they have never heard before? Will your illustrations be tailored to your audience or will it fit anyone who might hear your exposition of this portion of James? Will your sermon include material that might be controversial to one culture, but not to others? You must use homiletical skill to craft your sermon so that it is faithful to the text, but also sensitive to the ears of the listeners.

As you consider the following sermon, "Have You Got Good Religion," take note of the exegesis that underlies the exposition of James 1:26. Also, pay attention to the "homiletics" of the sermon.

## INTRODUCTION

One of the songs that I grew up hearing in the church asked a series of questions. The answer to each question was always "Certainly, Lord!"

"Have you been baptized?" "Certainly, Lord!"

"Is your name on high?" "Certainly, Lord!"

"Have you got good religion?" "Certainly, Lord!"

The chorus was "Certainly, certainly, certainly, Lord!"

I can't help but think that if James, the half brother of the Lord Jesus Christ, was in our midst, he would ask the question to each of us, "Have you got good religion?" It's possible that the question might shock you. You might answer the servant of Jesus Christ by saying, "James, don't you know that Christianity is a relationship, not a religion?"

Once the initial shock is over, you will probably remember that James's letter to the Christian Jews who have been scattered like seed is all about spiritual wholeness. James writes about a faith that is genuine and authentic. This faith displays itself in what can be called "good religion." It is a religion that is not hypocritical. Such a person cannot be accused of being a fake.

A Christian cannot possess "good religion" unless he or she has a proper relationship with the Word of God. This is what James has been arguing in the larger context of our text. The believer must *listen* to God's Word (1:19–21). There must be *an eagerness to hear* the Word (1:19–20). There must also be at the entrance of one's heart *a welcome mat that accepts* the implanted Word with open arms (1:21).

The child of God must also *obey* God's word (1:22–25). It is not enough to be a hearer of the Word. The individual who only hears the Word and does not do it makes a serious miscalculation (1:22). The hearing of the Word minus doing it is as nonsensical as declaring that $2 + 2 = 5$. Failure to do the Word is as foolish as waking up in the morning and looking at yourself in the mirror, seeing your sleepy eyes. You see the sleep crust in the corner of your eyes. You also see the dry spit on the edge of your mouth. You even see that your huge afro is lopsided! Despite what you see, you do nothing about it (see 1:23–24).

The doer of the Word is favored and blessed by God (1:25). He looks intently into the Word. This individual lingers alongside of the Word. There is no forgetfulness of the Word for this person. Instead, by the Holy Spirit, the work of the Word that is seen in God's mirror, the Bible, is done.

Eager to hear God's Word and committed to practicing it—isn't that enough to prove that good religion requires a proper relationship with the Word? Not in the mind of James. There is a danger that obeying God's Word might simply be outward. It could be an obedience that characterized the young child who finally stopped playing with his toys and came to the dinner table after his mother demanded he do so. The smart aleck told his mother, "I may be sitting down, but in my heart I am still playing with my toys." There is no place for an obedience that does not touch the inner life. Good religion displays itself both internally and externally.

The question on the floor is, "Do you have good religion?" Before you answer, "Certainly, certainly, certainly, Lord," consider the words that James has written in 1:26–27. Two pictures of religion are provided to help the Christian to answer this crucial question.

## A Picture of Bad Religion (1:26)

There is a religion that is bad in God's eyes. The parable of the Pharisee and the Publican in Luke 18:9–14 testifies to this. Jesus tells us that two men went to the temple to pray. One is identified as a Pharisee, the other a Publican (tax gatherer).

The Pharisee's prayer reveals how highly he thought of himself. He was not a swindler, unjust, an adulterer, or even like the tax gatherer. His "religiosity" showed up in fasting twice a week and paying tithes of all that he got. Yet, his religion was not acceptable to God. Jesus declared that this man did not go down to his house justified. In other words, he possessed bad religion that left him in his sins.

To help us determine if we have bad religion, James provides us with a photograph of it. Instead of using the mirror of God's Word, the servant of God and the Lord Jesus Christ puts before us a snapshot. A close look at this picture reveals the marks of a religion that is unacceptable to God.

### Bad Religion Looks Religious

There is a religion that is merely external. It is a religion that will result in a person spending eternity in the lake of fire. Bad religion will be characteristic of the last days that Paul mentions in 2 Timothy 3:5. Individuals will hold to a form of godliness, even though they will deny its power. It was a religion that Jesus addressed in His famous Sermon on the Mount. The Lord stated, "For I say to you that unless your righteousness surpasses that of the scribes and Pharisees, you will not enter the kingdom of heaven" (Matt. 5:20 NASB).[2] There is a righteousness that is unacceptable. It will not allow an individual to enter heaven.

The characteristics of bad religion are introduced to

---

2. The NASB is used throughout this chapter unless noted otherwise.

the readers by means of a hypothetical situation. The hypothetical situation, introduced by the word "if," involves a person named "anyone." This person is called "anyone" because the situation that is about to be described might fit any of the readers of the letter of James. The identity of "anyone" is left indefinite in order to communicate to the readers that if the shoe fits, wear it.

The person named "anyone" thinks he is religious. He is of the opinion that he worships God. As he considers his activities, he concludes that he has a personal relationship with God. He is a regular church attender. He leads the morning devotions before the worship service. He is the first one in the "Tither's Line." His prayers are majestic and takes you around the whole world and to every hospital. There is no question in this person's mind that he is right with God. He does all of the outward acts that are required. He thinks he is religious since he performs the religious duties.

### Bad Religion Is Powerless

Even though "Mr. Anyone" thinks he is religious, at the same time he "does not bridle his tongue." In other words, he's got loose lips. The words that come out of his mouth can't be controlled. With his tongue he praises God, and with that same tongue he curses those who are made in God's image (3:9–12).

James portrays the tongue as a wild horse that needs a bit and bridle to be kept under control. A "bridle" was a piece of iron that was placed in the horse's mouth to check and guide it, to harness the power of a horse.

The half brother of the Lord looks into the mouth of

this man who thinks he is religious and notices that there is no bridle. There is no metal piece of iron in this person's mouth that controls his tongue. James sees a tongue that is uncontrolled, unrestrained, and is free to do what it pleases. So while "Mr. Anyone" is doing his religious duties, he does not keep a tight rein on his tongue. In other words, there is a lack of control that is reflected in the use of the person's tongue.

In the mind of James, the tongue is more dangerous than a gun. Many in our day are advocates of "gun control." *James is an advocate of "tongue control."* The tongue is capable of deceiving, lying, gossiping, slandering, exaggerating, flattering, boasting, murmuring, arguing, cursing, and more. The tongue has destroyed friendships, marriages, churches, and even nations. No day goes by where someone is not hurt by the tongue!

The half brother of the Lord provides an exposition on tongue control in 3:1–12. The tongue must be controlled since it is a barometer of spiritual maturity (3:1–2). It is powerful (3:3–5), it is destructive (3:6–12), and it is inconsistent (3:9–12).

A failure to control the tongue is a sign that bad religion is powerless. It is unable to help when it comes to "tongue control." There is clearly no bit and bridle in the mouth of the one who possesses bad religion.

### Bad Religion Is Deceptive

In strong contrast to "Mr. Religion" not bridling his tongue is the reality that this person "deceives his *own* heart." It is not stated that he deceives others. Rather, he deceives the very core of his being—his *heart.* Tragically, the deception is deep down within this person's real self.

The heart is the mission control center. It is the core of one's being. It is the place out of which come "evil thoughts, murders, adulteries, fornications, thefts, false witness, slanders" as declared by Jesus in Matthew 15:19. "Mr. Anyone" might "honor" God with his lips, but his heart is far from God. *He worships God in vain.*

The heart of "Mr. Religion" has hoodwinked him. It has tricked and deceived him. His heart has pulled him aside on a downtown street and showed him a bunch of nice-looking watches. It leads him to buy one of those watches—only to find out later that what he bought was a fake. It was not the real thing. The glistening "diamonds" were not real.

This individual is a living example of the words of the prophet Jeremiah to the nation of Israel. Jeremiah proclaimed, "The heart is more deceitful than all else and is desperately sick; who can understand it?" (Jer. 17:9). The sick heart of the man who thinks himself to be religious has deceived him and played a trick upon him.

Bad religion does that. It makes you think that you are right with God. Yet, you have been deceived. Throughout the pages of Scripture, both in the Old Testament and New Testament, individuals have been duped into thinking they have good religion, when in reality they have bad religion.

### Bad Religion Is Worthless

James takes his pen and writes the word "worthless" across the religion of "Mr. Anyone." The religion of this man is vain. It is futile. It is profitless and useless. Such a religion has no worth or any value. It will keep "Mr. Religion" out of heaven. The words that he will hear from the Lord Jesus Christ is "I never knew you; depart from Me, you who practice lawlessness" (Matt. 7:23). Even though he might acknowledge Jesus with the right title, "Lord, Lord," he will not enter heaven. Even though he might have performed spectacular feats like prophesying, casting out demons, and performing miracles in Jesus' name, his religion is useless before Christ. Religion that is external and not internal is unacceptable. Useless religion touches the outside of the person and leaves the inner person unchanged. There is reformation, but no transformation. It will leave a person dead in his trespasses and sins.

## A Picture of Good Religion

The picture of bad religion is not pretty. In fact, it is outright ugly. God looks into the face of bad religion and sees ugliness. He is disgusted with bad religion. He thoroughly detests it.

James removes from our eyes the picture of bad religion. He replaces it with a second picture that is incredibly different. It is a beautiful portrait of good religion. It is a painting of the kind of religion that meets God's approval. Not all religion is useless.

### Good Religion Is Pure

Good religion is not worthless. It is not dirty. Instead, it is described as "pure." It is morally clean. It reflects godly behavior. This kind of religion comes from a heart that is right before God and has been changed by the truths of God.

When I teach in a classroom or seminar setting, I periodically use PowerPoint slides. There are two slides that I like to use if my subject matter is living a clean and pure life.

The first slide shows a male child in a bathtub. His skin is wet with water and bubbles. He is holding over his head a cup that contains water. The picture shows the beautiful child pouring the water on the top of the head while he has a big grin on his face. He is the picture of cleanliness.

In stark contrast to the first picture is another slide that contains a picture of four kids, ages eight to ten. They are in their swimming suits. What is astounding about the picture is that they are playing in the mud. They, too, are smiling and are enjoying themselves, but from head to toe, each of them is dirty.

The contrast in these pictures portrays the difference between good and bad religion. A religion that is good is pristine.

### Good Religion Is Undefiled

Not only is good religion pure, it is also "undefiled." In order to stress the absolute cleanness of good religion, James adds this further description of the religion he has in mind. This religion is not stained or soiled due to contact with moral evil. The religion that James describes in 1:27 is free from pollution and contamination. It is the religion of a person who is pure in heart. There is nothing dirty or corrupt about good religion. When you get close to this kind of religion there are no surface stains or contaminates.

Pure and undefiled are attributes of good religion. It is a religion that passes God's evaluation. James declares it is acceptable "in the sight of *our God* and Father." You will not find this religion in the gutter. Instead, it is found in very presence of God because it is acceptable to Him. The God that James has in mind is not an impersonal God. He is the God who is "Father" to James, to the readers, and to every believer.

God's opinion is what matters when it comes to religion. James is not concerned with the opinion of one's father and mother or brother and sister. The evaluation of the pastors or the preachers is not his chief concern. At this point, it does not even matter what the deacons, deaconesses, and the mothers of the church think. Only God's evaluation matters. There is a religion that God accepts as pure and undefiled.

### Good Religion Manifests Itself in Love

The description of good religion gives way to its deeds. The focus is no longer on the attributes of a living faith but rather on the activities of such a faith. It can be said of good religion that it manifests itself in love. James puts it this way: "To visit orphans and widows in their distress." A distinguishing activity of acceptable religion is the practice of compassion.

Someone might hear the term "visit" and get the wrong impression. We use the word, and the idea of a social call fills our minds. The term was used in classical Greek of a friend or doctor who visited the sick. In the Greek version of the Old Testament, it referred to visiting a person with the aim of caring for that individual and supplying their needs. The Lord used this term in Matthew 25:36. He commends those who visited the least of His children, when they were sick. To "visit" is more than just a social occasion. The bottom line is that "visit" means to come to the aid of a needy individual.

The individuals selected for personal care and genuine visitation are "orphans and widows." An "orphan" was a child who had no parents. A "widow" was a woman who had experienced the death of her husband. The two groups together represent people who needed help. Sympathy and compassion were to be extended to them in light of their worth despite their condition. They were to be shown love as image bearers of God. Sadly, these individuals can be the object of exploitation.

Orphans and widows are linked together in the Old Testament. God said, "Defend the orphan, plead for the widow" (Isa. 1:17). The Law declared, "You shall not afflict any widow or orphan" (Ex. 22:22). One of the sins of Israel mentioned in Ezekiel is that "the fatherless and the widow they have wronged" (Ezek. 22:7).

Although an orphan was without parents and a widow was without a husband, they were not without the God of heaven and earth. Psalm 68:5 declares, "A father of the fatherless and a judge for the widows, is God in His holy habitation." Those who possess genuine religion are to copy their heavenly Father in showing love to orphans and widows. The time when this love is to be shown is when these individuals are in the midst of distress. Turbulence and affliction will cross the paths of these cherished individuals. When they do, those who possess authentic religion will be like a caring doctor to them.

### Good Religion Manifests Itself in Holiness

A religion that is pure and undefiled also manifests itself in holiness. This kind of religion has a social dimension as well as an ethical one. It demonstrates itself horizontally in relation to others and vertically in relation to God.

A distinguishing activity of godly religion is to "keep oneself unstained by the world." The person who practices this kind of religion is diligent to guard himself. He keeps watch over himself. There is a continual attentiveness with regard to his life. He is not slothful or lazy in his pursuit and practice of holiness.

This practitioner of good religion keeps a vigil regarding his life so that it is not soiled or stained. He realizes that "the world" has the ability to morally pollute. The "world" that is referred to is not the world of people. Nor is it the world of creation. James uses this term in the same way that some of the New Testament writers do. The "world" is the organized system of evil that is headed by Satan (see 1 John 5:19), is made up of unbelievers, and has values and beliefs that leave God out. In light of this, the world is to Satan what the church is to Christ. The Christian is to view the world in this sense as an enemy and not a friend (see James 4:4). Christians are not to love the world (1 John 2:15). Nor are they to be conformed to it (Rom. 12:1–2). Rather, they are to be on the alert so that they remain unspotted by it.

During my time as a seminary professor, I had the privilege of meeting with small groups of students each semester. Our discipleship group was designed to help students grow in godliness. At the conclusion of the six-week class, I would take them to a well-known local barbeque restaurant. I wanted them to enjoy some good barbeque. Of course, in the name of ministry, I wanted to enjoy it also. The various meats came on platters filled with sauce. The challenge for each of us was not to allow the sauce to stain our shirts. We were not always successful. There were times when a shirt was spotted by the barbeque sauce.

The one who possesses good religion is successful by God's grace in keeping oneself away from the stains and spots produced by the world. He lives a morally pure life. He is like the writer of Psalm 119, who realized that the path to a morally clean life is to guard one's life by using the standard of God's Word (see Ps. 119:9).

Good religion is a balanced religion. It is marked by both love and holiness. Some evangelicals have forgotten this, stressing the importance of love to the neglect of holiness. This love manifests itself in compassion for the social needs of others. There is a concern for the homeless. Food is regularly provided for the hungry. They remember those in prison as though in prison with them. All of these activities are valid expressions of the love that James speaks of when he says that godly religion visits orphans and widows in their distress. Yet there have been times when compassion has been stressed at the expense of holiness. A strong concern for one's neighbor has resulted in loose living.

Other evangelicals stress holiness to the neglect of love. There is a strong emphasis on the believer's vertical relationship to God. Piety and godliness is highlighted. An intellectual knowledge of the Bible is what matters most. Great theology and sound doctrine is touted for these Christians. In the midst of these wonderful activities, love for one's neighbor is often forgotten. They honor the great and foremost commandment to love God with all of their heart, soul, mind, and strength (Matt. 22:37–38). But, they have forgotten that there is another commandment that is like the greatest one. They do not love others as they do themselves (Matt. 22:39).

One should remember that James is not an advocate of an "either/or" but a "both/and" approach when it comes to love and holiness. Pure and undefiled religion manifests itself in both visiting orphans and widows in their distress and in keeping oneself unspotted from the world. Religion that pleases God fleshes itself out in charity and chastity, in sympathy and separation, and in compassion and cleanness.

## Close

Have you got good religion? An honest answer to that question requires a close look at the two pictures of religion that are presented in James 1:26–27.

There is a religion that is not good. Bad religion looks religious, lacks power, and is deceptive. It is worthless. The person who possesses it will spend eternity in the lake of fire. If your look at the snapshot of bad religion reveals that you've got bad religion, then you need to be saved. Empty religion doesn't become acceptable religion by human effort. It springs from a brand new heart that is given to you when you trust in Jesus Christ alone for salvation.

Good religion is pure and undefiled. It is acceptable to almighty God. This religion manifests itself in love and holiness.

*Have you got good religion?* My prayer is that you can answer "Certainly, certainly, certainly, Lord!"

## CONCLUSION

Let's analyze the sermon section-by-section with the goal of identifying some of the exegetical and homiletical decisions that were made.

In the introduction, the attention of the intended audience was captured via a song commonly sung in African American churches. Although the song might not be familiar to all of the audience, the questions that the song asks serve as an attention grabber. The introduction also addressed the matter of Christianity not being a religion, but a relationship. It is important that the audience understands James's use of "religion." Furthermore, the introduction specified the relationship of the three sections (1:19–21; 1:22–25; 1:26–27). Finally, the introduction highlighted the structure of 1:26–27. Maybe you missed it. The structure was introduced under the umbrella that the two verses provide two pictures of religion.

The section "A Picture of Bad Religion" reveals several decisions made regarding exegesis and exposition. It dealt with the "if" statement of verse 26. The interpretive option of "thinks" rather than "seems" was chosen. The illustrations connected to "Mr. Anyone" are relevant to those exposed to "traditional" African American churches. The relationship of the participle "bridle" to the main verb "thinks" indicated that both of these actions took place at the same time. In fact, the term "bridle" was defined. The conjunction "but" was expressed as indicating a strong contrast. The audience was given the meaning of both "deceive" and "vain." The picture of bad religion was portrayed as religious, powerless,

198

deceptive, and worthless. This portrait was not manufactured out of the air but produced from the text. This picture was based upon the words and phrases "religious," "does not bridle," "deceives," and "worthless." This allows the text to determine the structure of the message.

Hopefully you were alert to the various interpretive and homiletical concerns in the section of the sermon labeled "A Picture of Good Religion." The word "pure" was defined and illustrated. The hearer of the sermon was not left in the dark regarding the meaning of "undefiled." The preposition rendered "in the sight of" was taken as legitimate and was also explained. Sensitivity was shown in comments related to the African American church. Terms like "deacons," "deaconesses," and even "mothers" were used for well-known figures in these churches. Important words like "visit," "orphans," "widows," "keep," and "world" were defined. The tense of "keep" was brought out by saying an individual is to continually keep oneself unspotted from the world. The important relationship between "love" and "holiness" received necessary treatment. This section once again was structured in light of terms and phrases used in verse 27. It resulted in good religion being painted as pure, undefiled, manifesting itself in love, and manifesting itself in holiness.

The "Conclusion" portion of the sermon summarizes the contents of the sermon. It also appropriately asks the question, "Have you got good religion?" The prayerful wish of the preacher is that the intended audience can answer "Certainly, certainly, certainly, Lord."

An analysis of this sermon has revealed the importance of exegesis and homiletics in the exposition of God's Word.

# CHAPTER 11

# WAITING FOR A WEDDING

*Expository Preaching from the Apocalypse*

## REVELATION 21
## K. EDWARD COPELAND

On October 21, 2017, I was privileged to preach the closing message at the Charles Simeon Trust Workshop on Biblical Exposition hosted by Hinson Baptist Church in Portland, Oregon. The Charles Simeon Trust was founded in January 2001 by David Helm, Jon Dennis, and Kent Hughes. It was named for Charles Simeon, an evangelical and trainer of preachers in Cambridge, England, who ministered for fifty-four challenging years. Simeon Trust workshops are inspired by and modeled after those of Dick Lucas and the Proclamation Trust in London. What makes these workshops unique is that, over the course of three days, students work through an entire book of the Bible in small group settings where they present their preassigned homework, in large group settings where they are given principles and strategies for sound biblical exposition, and worship settings where they sit under the Word as it is preached by the instructors.

The title of the workshop in Portland was, "Preaching Apocalyptic Literature," and Revelation was the book we were working through. I was assigned to preach the entire chapter of Revelation 21 as the closing session of the workshop.

I arrived at the emphasis of the passage by paying close attention to how John structured his description of the scene before him. The passage naturally divides into two large parts with the first section starting with the phrase "Then I saw . . ." (v. 1 ESV),[1] and the second section beginning with "Then came one of the seven angels . . ." (v. 9). Thematically, the emphasis of the first section as revealed by the word pictures is on God's intimacy with His people. The emphasis in the second section is on the city that has been prepared for God's people, a description that includes a peculiar emphasis on what's missing in the city.

After discovering the emphasis by discerning the structure, I arrived at the meaning by employing exegetical principles and tools. Apocalyptic literature by its nature is evocative, visual, and visceral. Consequently, I focused on what the images were designed to convey and how they were intended to make the reader feel. I employed biblical theology to show how various themes and images can be traced from their beginnings in the Old Testament to their culmination in Revelation (for example, creation, marriage, and the tabernacle). I did word studies, cultural/historical background studies, and contextual studies to test my understanding of what this text would have meant to its original hearers. After some theological reflection on what the passage meant in light of the death, burial, and resurrection of Christ, I crafted my homiletical outline.

Since both sections of chapter 21 and the immediately preceding chapters have the language of marriage featured prominently

---

1. The ESV is used throughout this chapter unless otherwise noted.

and the passage was designed to comfort its readers with the anticipation of a brand new cosmos where intimacy with God would be consummated, I settled on "Waiting for a Wedding" as the title of the sermon.

## INTRODUCTION

A popular thing now in my area is destination weddings—a couple decides to get married in a particular exotic spot, and everybody has to go meet them there. I've missed a few of these weddings because I didn't have the funds to travel to the exotic location, but I enjoy seeing the postcards and the wedding pictures. I wish I could have gone to several that have taken place in this last year. But I'm grateful to God that there's one wedding I'm not going miss. Our reservation has already been made. I'm longing to go to a place called "home" that I've never visited.

We've been working hard the last couple of days. I don't know about you, but lots of things are swirling about in my mind; a lot of images are coming to me. This orchestra called "Revelation" has so many notes and so many themes. We are coming here to the coda where we finally see the culmination of a lot of themes that did not start in Revelation but started all the way back in Genesis. Themes and concepts that have appeared all throughout Scripture now bring us to this final culmination. There is so much in here. However, in light of what I believe the Holy Spirit is saying to you and me, I want to just focus on this wedding that we're waiting for in the city in which we will be satisfied.

You can approach this passage from several different

angles. If you were to take a look at Genesis 1 and the creation account, or even compare Genesis 1 to what we see here, you would see that just as God created light then, so He is the light now. Genesis revealed day and night, but now there is no more night. Or you could think about how there is creation in Genesis 1 and then a marriage in Genesis 2; and now, at the end of Revelation, having explored movements through various genres of literature, through various expressions of the theme of God's grace being played out in so many different ways, we have a *new* creation and *another* wedding.

## Exposition

*Newness*

So let's see if we can dig down for just a second. John starts out in verse 1, saying "Then I saw. . . ." Now as you walk through this passage, you are going to hear him say "I saw" at various points. He saw several different things. But it's interesting that he starts out by saying he saw a new heaven and a new earth. That word "new" means a completely different type, a completely different character, a new nature. This is not *renovation*; this is replacement. John says the first heavens and the first earth have passed away.

God is *recreating* the cosmos and He has started something brand new. After John talks about this idea of a new earth, he focuses the rest of the chapter on a city, a *new* city.

John focuses on the people that make up this new city, the New Jerusalem. They are the bride of Christ. We've already seen the wedding back in chapter 19. We just studied it in the words, "Blessed are those who are invited to the marriage supper of the Lamb" (Rev. 19:9). Here we are in chapter 21, and John is speaking of Jerusalem as one who is made ready as a bride adorned for her husband.

### Bride

As we look at these first few verses, I would like to impress upon your heart the images of *intimacy* that are prevalent in this text and that give our heart cause to rejoice—for what we see in the pixels now we will see in person then. So the first image is this bride. Now that starts out in Genesis: the man and the woman were naked and not ashamed, and they become one, so on and so forth.

If you traced this type of imagery all the way through Scripture, you would find that God wants to have intimacy with His people. This is reflected in passages like Isaiah 54:5, where God is said to be the husband of His people of Israel. We find similar themes in the Song of Solomon. We also find images that express God's faithfulness despite our faithlessness (or our idolatry) in books like Hosea. We also find this concept of intimacy in the New Testament, most notably in Ephesians 5, where we learn that even our earthly marriages are designed to point to something else—the relationship with Christ has with His church.

All along, God has wanted to be intimate with us, and one day that intimacy will be culminated in an unfiltered, unrestricted way as we, His bride, finally see Him face-to-face and are able to enjoy His presence as fully redeemed people.

*Tabernacle*

The bride is not the only image of intimacy here. In verse 3, we read, "Behold, the tabernacle of God is among men, and He will dwell among them" (NASB). Tabernacle here means "tent." What was the original tabernacle designed to be? A place that was movable but where God could meet with His people—where He could pitch His tent and dwell among His people.

You can trace the tabernacle-tent idea and temple theology all throughout Scripture. The point is that God wants to meet with us and there's a place that He's designated to do that. In Revelation 21, it is in this new heavens and new earth—not a renovated earth but a redesigned cosmos. God is going to pitch His tent with us. He is going to dwell with us. We will be His people, and He Himself will be among us! How much closer can we get? How much more intimacy can there be? It's not a camping trip; it's His covering over us. The image is one of His protection of us in an intimate setting.

However, it is not just the tabernacle that represents intimacy. Verse 4 says that He will wipe every tear from their eyes. The intimacy reflected in this image is that of a husband and a wife. God is not just pitching His tent among us. God is so tender and compassionate that *He Himself* will wipe away all our tears—everything that causes us to cry. He's going to deal with these things because He's making everything brand new! What was broken back in Genesis and what has caused us consternation, misery, and pain all throughout the ages, now in this new heaven and new earth, will be removed forever! What I'm waiting on is this wedding where I get to see Jesus face-to-face, where

His banner over me will be love (see Song 2:4), and where He will wipe away every tear from my eye. That's what I'm waiting on; it is a picture of intimacy. What about you?

After John sees and hears these things, the angel then says, in effect, "John, let me help you understand that the bride is the wife of the Lamb, and she has a *place* that has been prepared for her—a place to which I want to carry you away for a virtual tour."

### City

If God gives me grace and someone gives me money, I plan on going to Italy this winter with my daughter. I told her, "I'll take you anywhere you want to go once in your lifetime." She said, "Italy!" I said, "Let's go!"

I have an Italian friend who has put together little packets and sent me video clips of virtual tours. I've never been there. I've always wanted to go. I'm on my way. And I'm excited now because I keep getting glimpses.

The angel basically said to John, "Let me take you on a virtual tour." John writes, "And he carried me away in the Spirit to a great, high mountain, and showed me the holy city Jerusalem coming down out of heaven from God" (21:10). Then the angel starts describing some things, all of which have allusions to Old Testament passages like Ezekiel 48 and some places in Isaiah. You can even argue, as some scholars try to argue, that the precious stones that are used have specific reference to things like some of the artistry or priestly garb in the first temple. All of that sounds interesting.

I think what is really going on here is that John, even as he describes all these things, is letting us know that this place is more glorious than we can imagine! The best things we have here on earth are things we just used to pave the streets in heaven.

Now there's more meaning as relates to the twelve gates, the twelve angels, the twelve tribes of Israel, the twelve foundation stones, and the twelve apostles (vv. 11–14). Seemingly, all of this is talking about the fullness of God's people. Yes, that's true and that's important. But I think the visual portrayal is that this place is so out of this world that you can barely imagine it, because the best stuff we have around here in this present world doesn't even come close to what is waiting for us. That is the place that He has designed for us.

What makes the place desirable is not just its description but it's what's missing. In the new heaven and earth, there is not going to be any sea. Various scholars argue about what this means. In Scripture, the sea often represents chaos and evil. So I think he is saying that there will be no environment for evil to flourish in this new place.

John also says that there will no longer be any death: no mourning or no crying, because God has made all things brand new! Verse 8 talked about the fact that cowardly, unbelieving, abominable murderers, liars, sorcerers, idolaters, and immoral persons won't be there. And in verse 22, we find that there is no temple in this place. Why not? The city is laid out in a square. It's length and height and width are equal. The only other place in the Bible we see these kind of descriptions is the Holy of Holies—the *most* intimate place in the temple. But now there is no need for a temple because the whole place is where we will have unmediated, unfiltered, unrestricted intimacy with God. The whole city is a temple. There's no need for any temple because the Lord God Almighty and the Lamb are its temple. We do not need any sun or any moon because God illumines it and the Lamb is the lamp.

### Nations

This is a reference we see here to Isaiah 60, which speaks about the nations and their kings, who will bring all their glory to Jerusalem. You know how ancient kings would bring their retinue. Think of the Queen of Sheba, who came to visit Solomon and brought gifts of tribute. That's what kings and queens did; they brought gifts to the cities they visited. In this heavenly city, the kings of the earth will bring all their glory, their tribute, to the city.

Verse 27 says that nothing unclean and no one who practices abomination can get into the city. This is a restrictive, private, exclusive party or wedding reception—exclusive in the sense that only those who accepted the invitation can get in. You can't just show up if you didn't RSVP. The invitation is to all, but only those who respond to the invitation are able to get in.

## Application

So what does all this have to do with you and me? There's a whole lot more in this text, and you have been given the tools to dig it all out. I just want to focus on the intimacy in the place prepared for us.

Given the fact that there's a wedding that we have to get ready for—that there is a place being prepared for us—how ought we to live? How ought we conduct ourselves as men of God who have been tasked to preach the Word of God? The fact that we have a calling does not excuse us from working out our convictions in our daily behavior in light of where we're going.

My wife of twenty-eight years, Starla, is a beautiful woman. When I first started courting her, she lived in Oakland, California. I was living in Kankakee, Illinois. She sent me a *picture* of herself. This is ancient history. We used to call those pictures a "Kodak." This was back when a "picture" was a physical thing that you would place in another physical thing called a "photo album." She sent me a picture with a letter telling of her love for me, and I kept this picture with me everywhere I would go. When I would drive, I would have the picture in the sun visor, and at stops I would pull the picture down. The picture and the promises she made in those letters are what kept me from looking at other women, and kept me from doing things that perhaps I would have done otherwise. I couldn't—and didn't want to—do them because I was waiting on a wedding. And there is still somebody who wants to be intimate with me, so that means I have to cut off all of these others. I have to find ways to make sure that I'm maintaining an exclusive intimacy.

Brothers, in light of the realities that we see depicted in this chapter, should we not live a certain way? Consider how John says it: "Dear friends, now we are children of God, and what we will be has not yet been made known. But we know that when Christ appears, we shall be like him, for we shall see him as he is" (1 John 3:2 NIV). It's not just my behavior that should be my concern; it is my attitude that also needs to be submitted to God. Sometimes you can be doing the right thing but lack the right attitude.

When our twenty-fifth anniversary was coming up, I happened to be enrolled in a class at Trinity Evangelical

Divinity School. One of the wise brothers in the class asked me, "So what are you going to do for your twenty-fifth anniversary?" I said, "I think I'm going to surprise my wife and take her on a trip wherever she wants to go." He said, "That would be alright, but I have a better idea." So I asked, "What is it?" He said, "Tell her where you're taking her."

Our anniversary is in August, and this happened in November of the previous year. But he repeated, "Tell her where you're going to take her." So I asked why, and he said, "Because you can get credit for where you are getting ready to go." I said, "Man, you are good! That's a great idea."

So I took his advice and I asked my wife where she would like to go for the anniversary. She said, "Hawaii." So I said, "If you want to go to Hawaii, I'm taking you to Hawaii for our anniversary!" This was still back in November.

Now guess what: There were times in the intervening months, even though we are in an intimate marriage relationship, when our attitude wasn't quite *warm*. My wife and I live in the Midwest. We get an attitude when it's cold outside for a long time. At those times, I would say to my wife, "Hawaii in August." Her whole attitude would change. Sometimes we would have disagreements or whatever, but we would make up quickly, and I would get January sugar in anticipation of an August Hawaii.

What's your attitude as it relates to the One that we've been betrothed to and the One we're waiting to wed? Do you know what is waiting for you, and can you let that inform your attitude now?

I know you have to go back to the situation you left behind for this conference. Maybe the elders are giving you a headache, or maybe you're one of the elders who is giving headaches. Maybe you're bi-vocational and you're feeling overwhelmed. You see the work that you have to do and are asking yourself, "Man, how can I do it all?" Maybe you're trying to keep in step with the Holy Spirit even though you don't know what you're going to be doing in the next few months.

Listen, the promise is not Hawaii, but *heaven*: Let that inform your reality now. Let where are you going help you with your attitude where you are right now. If you know payday is Friday, you can get through Wednesday because you know Friday is on the way.

We're waiting on a wedding, and there's a place that's been prepared for us—a place we've been longing for all our lives, a place we've never seen. And when we get there, what is so heavenly about heaven is not the stones, pearls, or gold, but that the One we've only seen glimpses of will actually be there for us to be intimate with. That hope right now helps us not only to do the right thing, but to have the right attitude while doing it. Don't be overwhelmed; you can do it all in light of the fact that there is One who *loves* you.

## Close

There's a hymn I used to like to sing that said,

> O I want to see him, look upon his face,
> there to sing forever of his saving grace;
> on the streets of Glory let me lift my voice;
> cares all past, home at last, ever to rejoice.[2]

---

2. R. H. Cornelius, "Oh, I Want to See Him" (1916), Hymnary.org, https://hymnary .org/text/as_i_journey_through_the_land_singing_as.

You ain't home yet; we're resident aliens. That is not a cause for despair but a cause for rejoicing. One day, we will be at the wedding supper of the Lamb, without spot or wrinkle, and we will enjoy His unfiltered face in the place He has prepared for us forever and ever. Amen.

## CONCLUSION

I faced several challenges in preaching this passage. One challenge was the length of the passage. If I were preaching to a typical congregation in an ordinary Sunday morning setting, I would not have chosen to preach the entire chapter in one setting. The Simeon Trust organizers chose the passage and its length. It was my obligation to preach the whole thing. I appreciated the challenge because it forced me to be more focused on what was most important to communicate. Because the passage was long and the imagery was dense, I had to make several editing decisions lest this sermon on eternal matters last an eternity itself.

Another challenge was the audience. I was preaching to preachers and, therefore, had to decide on how to apply the passage in a way that was preacher specific. My stated assignment was to preach to encourage the brothers and not necessarily to preach a model sermon. Of course, every sermon ought to be as excellent as it can be. Every sermon ought to exhort as well. I had to attend to sound exposition without trying to show off and encourage brothers who were preparing to go back out to the battlefield without being overly academic. It was after lunch at the end of an intense three-day immersion in apocalyptic literature. I tried to be crisp, clear, concise, and conversational so as to send them away refreshed even if they were not impressed.

One of the greatest challenges in preaching this passage was not to get bogged down in every detail of imagery. There were so many vivid word pictures and so many details that begged for explanation it was hard not to chase rabbits. Ultimately, I did my best to stick with the emphasis the structure revealed to me and to reflect the imagery in my contemporary examples and illustrations.

# PART 4

---

# Conclusion

CHAPTER 12

# A CASE FOR A REGULAR DIET OF PREACHING THROUGH A BIBLICAL BOOK

## ERIC C. REDMOND

As a whole the Scriptures are God's revealing Word. Only in the infiniteness of its inner relationships, in the connection of Old and New Testaments, of promise and fulfillment, sacrifice and law, law and gospel, cross and resurrection, faith and obedience, having and hoping, will the full witness to Jesus Christ the Lord be perceived.[1]

Dietrich Bonhoeffer's insight about the Scriptures and "the full witness of Jesus Christ" is an appropriate place to discuss what we are doing week after week, month after month, and year after year in heralding God's Word each Sunday, or maybe at least what we *should* be doing. The Lordship of Christ in and over every aspect of our lives, and of our church life as a corporate body, depends upon our reception of what all of Scripture says about Christ. It rests on the Holy Spirit of God opening our understanding of the truth of Scripture so that we can grasp how God fulfills

---

1. Dietrich Bonhoeffer, *Life Together: The Classic Exploration of Christian Community* (New York: Harper One, 1954), 51.

Old Testament promises in the New Testament and witness His faithfulness. It stands on the joy of discovering infinite "inner relationships"—spoken directly, figuratively, or mysteriously—all pointing to Jesus Christ: *Christ promised, Christ fulfilling, Christ typified in sacrifice, Christ as the one to obey with the Law, Christ the true standard of the Law, Christ the hope for those who fail the Law, Christ crucified for our redemption, Christ raised for our justification, Christ the giver of faith and worker of obedience, Christ presently ours now known in part as through as mirror dimly, and Christ known fully when the perfect comes.*

Preaching all the Scriptures is a means for presenting the full witness of Christ rather than only select portions. It is a means for presenting Christ as Lord of all things small and great, personal and familial, individual and corporate, private and societal, financial and sexual, educational and occupational, marital and parental, recreational and medical, pleasurable and painful, explainable and questionable, of things past and present and to come. The best way to give our people the wealth of the truth of Christ for all aspects of their lives is to preach through full books of the Bible as the majority of the regular diet of our preaching.

## What I Mean by "Regular Diet"

I am arguing for one means of growing a congregation and making the Word of God central to worship and the lives of God's people. There are other means and other proposals. I am making a case for beginning a preaching series with the first verse of a book of Scripture, in the first subunit of the many subunits that make up the full book, and continuing until you have finished preaching through the final subunit of the book. I am proposing that preaching Numbers, 2 Chronicles, Job, Psalms, Ezekiel, Nahum, Matthew,

Acts, 2 Corinthians, 2 Peter, Revelation, and all of the rest of the books of Scripture—from the opening section, pericope, episode, psalm, chapter, or other subunit of the whole book to the last—is the best way to make God's voice known to a congregation.

I would suggest that where exposition through books is the occasional offering and not even 50 percent of an annual preaching calendar, the people in the pews are not being nourished from the Word of God as well as they could be. The saints will hear outstanding sermons—in many cases—and many theological and practical ones. But exposition through books offers a unique clarity to God's full voice speaking through the canon of Scripture. I say this because of the distinctive work we are doing as we are preaching through the various books of Scripture.

When preaching through the books of Scripture, first, *we are revealing the God who spoke His will into existence and still speaks.* It is not that the Lord speaks only on praise, blessing, overcoming pain, forgiveness, love, tithing, submission, and serving—common themes for preaching. He speaks on many more ideas that cover other arenas of life. I was reminded of this while preaching through Acts and discovering that Acts 28:1–10 is about *overcoming barbaric stereotypes*. While working through 2 Chronicles, I came to understand that chapter 29 concerns repairing the building *so as to* restore the worship—a message that complements Ezra 3, which is about restoring worship *before* focusing on the building.

Again, when preaching through Proverbs, one will eventually land in 27:3–7 and (hopefully) discern that it is about the wisdom of *being satisfied with difficult life situations*. We prevent our people from thinking the Bible is a manual for picking and choosing their favorite subjects when they hear Scripture speak from every passage. We are teaching our people to accept God's will as revealed and unfolded, and not to perceive God's will as popcorn pieces popping up here and there.

Second, *we are taking away the notion that the Bible is a self-help manual, or one that exists for us to select only a few topics to study*. In making a case for reading books for pleasure rather than duty, Alan Jacobs notes "this self-help, self-improvement model of reading seems deeply embedded in American cultural life."[2] In preaching a few books, we inadvertently communicate that the rest of the Bible (1) can be summed up in the few familiar verses, (2) is less important than the few selected, or (3) is irrelevant. Yet going back repeatedly to familiar or favorite passages, like Psalms 51, 100, or 150, will not give our people what other passages like Psalm 73 also can give them.

For example, Psalm 51 is about *David's seeking of God's mercy upon him after he committed grave sin*. Psalm 100 concerns *the call for all the earth to enter the Lord's presence with celebration*, and Psalm 150 speaks to *the praise of the Lord by all of creation*. However, the subject of Psalm 73 is *the psalmist's nearly complete falling into personal despair over the prosperity of the wicked*, and it speaks to *a believer's crisis of faith in the face of the apparent triumph of evil in society over the innocent*. Learning to deal with a crisis of faith is relevant to many believers who cannot make sense of their lives seeming less prosperous since the day they professed Christ compared to their prosperity prior to coming to Christ.

The commonly preached psalms, like 51, 100, and 150, do not sum up Psalm 73 or the other psalms, Jonah 1, Hebrews 10, or 2 John. All four of the messages of Psalms 51, 100, 150, and 73 contribute to the maturing of believers and the church, as do the

---

2. Alan Jacobs, *The Pleasures of Reading in an Age of Distraction* (New York: Oxford University Press), 11.

messages of the other 146 psalms. Preaching through the Psalms and other books helps move us away from what Bonhoeffer lamented as "hearing the word of God for this particular day":

> Almost all of us have grown up with the idea that the Scripture reading is only a matter of hearing the Word of God for this particular day. That is why for many the Scripture reading consists only of a few, brief, selected verses which are to form the guiding thought of the day. There can be no doubt that the daily Bible passages published by the Moravian Brethren, for example, are a real blessing to all who have ever used them. This was discovered by many to their grateful astonishment particularly during the church struggle. But there can be equally little doubt that brief verses cannot and should not take the place of reading the Scripture as a whole. The verse for the day is still not the Holy Scripture which will remain throughout all time until the Last Day. Holy Scripture is more than a watchword. It is also more than "light for today." It is God's revealed Word for all men, for all times. Holy Scripture does not consist of individual passages; it is a unit and is intended to be used as such.[3]

Third, *we are revealing a consistent process of interpretation through an author, a genre, a testament, and the canon.* When D. Martin Lloyd-Jones launched into his first sermon on Romans 14:1 within his series on Romans, he began by referring to an earlier sermon in the series and his exposition of an earlier text:

> You remember how, in the first two verses of the twelfth chapter, [Paul] introduces the whole practical section with the words [of Rom. 12:1-2]. And now we must start with those two verses because everything in the fourteenth chapter is really covered by that introduction.
>     What does the Apostle do in this practical section? Well, let me give you a hurried summary of chapters 12 and 13. He first of

---

3. Bonhoeffer, *Life Together*, 50–51.

all deals with our relationship with other members of the church in the matter of our spiritual gifts, showing how trouble and disharmony can arise through a failure to realize the truth concerning this teaching. . . . Then beginning at chapter 13, the Apostle gives valuable advice and teaching with regard to the important question of the relationship of the believer to "the powers that be" . . .

And, finally, the Apostle drives his teaching home and enforces it upon us by reminding us that our time in this world is very limited, very short. . . .

But now, in chapter 14, the Apostle takes up another matter; that is why I say that there is a new subsection here.[4]

As he picked up preaching Romans 14 as part of a series through the book, Lloyd-Jones was able to demonstrate consistency in the thought of Paul and consistency in his own belief. He also teaches his people how to read New Testament epistolary literature as he walks through the book weekly: "He introduces . . . gives valuable advice . . . takes up another matter." Finally, as Lloyd-Jones tells his people how he comes to his conclusions, he is inferring that his way to approach passages is the right way to approach passages, for as the people's shepherd, he would show them only what he believed was the right way to read Scripture and not the wrong way to read Scripture. The same could be said if one preaches through law, narrative, poetry, prophecy, and apocalyptic.

After years of sitting under expositions through books, people will notice consistencies in the interpretation of each testament—consistencies both internally within the testament itself and externally in comparison to the other testament. They will see how each passage in a book is part of the message of a whole book—that each passage is related to the ones before and after it, and that

---

4. D. M. Lloyd-Jones, *Romans: Exposition of Chapter 14:1-17: Liberty and Conscience* (Carlisle, PA: Banner of Truth, 2003), 1–3.

the Lord has one whole message with which to bless their lives through the book and many individual blessings in each subdivision you preach. Thus, the people will embrace the Scriptures as a work that can be interpreted with understanding.

Whatever the shepherd preaches weekly is the way the people learn to interpret any passage. If the pastor proclaims an eternal conscious torment in hell for the lost, the members learn to embrace the pastor's method of interpreting the passages that led to the conclusion. If, however, the shepherd justifies the eternal annihilation of the wicked in his preaching, the members learn to embrace the pastor's method of interpreting the passages that led to this alternative conclusion, even if the shepherd comes to his conclusion philosophically rather than exegetically. That is, if the shepherd says, "But these texts cannot promote eternal damnation and everlasting suffering because God is loving and merciful," those sitting under his weekly teaching learn to interpret with a priority on the character of God that is divorced from their reading of the immediate passage. This could be said of the interpretation of any passage: If one comes to paedobaptist conclusions in reading Genesis 17, the paedobaptist membership will accept such readings. If one comes to *woke* conclusions in reading Matthew 25, the congregation will learn to read Scripture with *wokeness*.

Additionally, while *revealing a consistent process of interpretation* through preaching to your people each Sunday, you are *taking advantage of the biggest educational hour and evangelistic hour in the church*. Teaching through books at a Bible study is good, but not nearly as many of your people come to Bible study, Sunday school, or small group. On Sunday morning, you have your greatest opportunity to provide biblical education to the majority of your congregation. In Sunday worship, whole families are hearing together the oracles of God and understanding how the Lord is

223

speaking one main idea through each book.

Unbelievers in your midst, too, are hearing God's voice as it unfolds from each successive passage. While preaching, you are speaking to people who may rarely return for Bible study. As the topics change weekly and conviction or guilt falls upon them, let them witness that God is telling you what to preach week to week according to the topics He already has deposited in Scripture. Allow them to witness that each topic of speaking is not according to your proclamation of preselected topics—of what might appear to the people as your choosing of topics, no matter how certain you are that the Holy Spirit guided your choice of topical study.[5]

Fourth, *we are modeling the biblical, spiritually formative discipline of studying the Scriptures*. I am not saying that topical preaching does not require study. Neither am I suggesting that one cannot model a habit of study while presenting topical sermons. Instead, I am recognizing that working through passages week to week and allowing the Spirit of God to illuminate the subject of the next unit of Scripture takes a different sort of discipline of study than does establishing a topic and then explaining the various passages on the topic. For example, if one offers a six-week series on prayer—for example, *Definition* (which would be a theological sermon since Scripture does not have a "definition" of prayer anywhere), *Adoration*, *Confession*, *Thanksgiving*, *Supplication*, and *Warfare*—the topic gives the focus of the sermon and the passages one will select. The

---

5. Karl Vaters proposes, "It's much easier to pastor someone that you're seeing three times a week. But when you only see them two or three times a month, the word 'pastoring' has to take on a different meaning.... When we have so little of people's time and attention, we must make the best of it. Training, mentoring, discipling and equipping must be Job One. And not just in small groups and discipleship classes. It needs to become the focus of our main Sunday services" ("Church Attendance Patterns Are Changing and We Have to Adapt," *Pivot: A Blog by Karl Vaters*, May 02, 2018, https://www.christianitytoday.com/karl-vaters/2018/may/church-attendance-patterns-are-changing-we-have-to-adapt.html?start=2).

work of determining the topic on which God speaks is completed. Various interpretive nuances and related theology will arise within the sermon. But the work of discovery is nearly done.

In contrast, when one preaches on prayer in the process of giving expositions of the Sermon on the Mount (Matt. 6:1–18), one studies differently after that sermon in order to preach next on *the explanation of the relationship between treasures and personal allegiances* from Matthew 6:19–25 or on *the disciple's decisions about the setting of his or her affections* from 6:19–34. Similarly, if one preaches on prayer from Acts 12, a different sort of study takes place to preach about *strong acts of judgment consistent with the preaching of the gospel* from Acts 13 the next week. The hearers will know this and learn to read their Scriptures the same way. As Jennifer Doverspike concludes about *reading* a whole book, "The complexity of a well-researched book takes you on a long walk with the author, who is making a well-reasoned argument over hundreds of pages. The time and effort taken to *read* the book is analogous to the time and effort to write it, which means you engage with the topic more fully, and themes and theses will begin repeating throughout."[6] *Preaching* through full books of Scripture and hearing preaching through whole books of Scripture equally provide such engagement with the voice of God.

## Why People Object to a Diet of Preaching through Books

Some say that such expository preaching is boring, redundant, irrelevant, and impractical. In the experiences of certain congregations,

---

6. Jennifer Doverspike, "Why You Should Absolutely Read a Whole Book This Year," *The Federalist*, February 27, 2017, http://thefederalist.com/2017/02/22/absolutely-read-whole-book-year/.

these charges might be true. But these charges are truthful relative to the *abilities of the expositor* to make great use of rhetoric, to be knowledgeable of current events, to be aware of the needs and concerns of his own people, and to be able to move from the theology on the page into the contemporary age. The problem is not with the concept of exposition through books of Scripture.

I find nothing inherently boring or irrelevant about expositions of Scripture, especially when the preacher ties the exposition to the gospel and to a powerful use of African American style and rhetoric in preaching. Instead, I think God constructed Scripture in such a manner as to warrant exposition through whole books of Scripture above all other proposals for weekly preaching. Scripture does not present itself as a series of topical ideas or relevant sound bites. It presents itself as a book of sixty-six books to be read, studied, pondered, understood, explained, obeyed, enjoyed, and memorized. Although this truth should be enough to establish a case for preaching through books regularly, it would be wise to address a few significant objections to this case.

First, for some preachers, *certain books in the Bible do not appear to be relevant in whole or in part*. I have never found a passage that was not "relevant." God is relevant to everything as Lord of all. His gospel is relevant to everything as the solution to humankind's plight before God. The good news of Jesus Christ provides our access to God, and God is the most relevant being there is. God Almighty should be the Person of the Year and the top news story of every year, so to speak.

I would suggest that the problem of the appearance of a lack of relevancy exists, in part, because we have been taught that only certain passages are relevant as we grew up hearing only selective passages. Yet the apostle Paul understood that the ancient Hebrew Scriptures, written from the fifteenth to the fifth century BC, were relevant to the concerns facing the church in the first century AD: "All Scripture is God-breathed and is useful for teaching, rebuking, correcting and training in righteousness, so that the servant of God may be thoroughly equipped for every good work" (2 Tim. 3:16–17).[7] Paul told Timothy to preach texts written for a theocratic nation hundreds and thousands of years before the church in Ephesus existed because those words were *"useful . . . for every* good work."

Second, other preachers might find *that preaching through books does not allow for flexibility in a series as the Spirit of God leads*. Actually, the choice on what to preach weekly always is before the preacher. You can jump out of your series if a Charleston, Ferguson, or Charlottesville happens.[8] In fact, you should. Or if you uncover a sex-parties ring among your singles or a growing epidemic of couples receiving harmful, cultlike advice for their marriages, then you have a responsibility to address the concerns. You are not serving the series. The series is serving you and the people.

Third, some preachers think *they will become bored or that their people will not give attention to a long series.* If you decide to preach Lloyd-Jones's length series through Romans or Philippians, you might bore your people, for they might not be able to see the

---

7. For similar sentiments about the relevancy of the ancient Old Testament Scriptures to those living contemporaneous to the New Testament authors, see Rom. 4:3; 15:4; 16:25–27; 1 Cor. 9:9–10; 10:6, 11; 1 Peter 1:10–12.

8. I am referring to the Charleston Church Massacre (2015), the Ferguson Unrest (2014), and the Charlottesville White Supremacy rally and protests (2017). See Nick Corasaniti, Richard Pérez-Peña, and Lizette Alvarez, "Church Massacre Suspect Held as Charleston Grieves," *New York Times,* June 18, 2015, https://www.nytimes.com/2015/06/19/us/charleston-church-shooting.html; Abby Phillip, "After Unarmed Teen Michael Brown Is Killed, the St. Louis Post-Dispatch Front Page Captures Ferguson Burning, *The Washington Post,* August 11, 2014, https://www.washingtonpost.com/news/post-nation/wp/2014/08/11/after-unarmed-teen-michael-brown-is-killed-the-st-louis-post-dispatch-front-page-captures-ferguson-burning/?utm_term=.4b3443844c14; and Eric C. Redmond, Walter J. Redmond Jr., and Charis A. M. Redmond, "#Charlottesville: Some Gospel Thinking on White Supremacy," *Themelios* 42.3 (2017): 494–504.

unity of the book's message over a series that seems unending. Certainly, we are wise to remember that we have an enemy who will distract and tell people that your preaching through a book for a long period is ridiculous.

You, however, can preach larger chunks (for example, Matthew in ten sermons as a large overview rather than in twenty-eight or fifty sermons, or the Psalms in fifteen sermons as representative of a tenth of the Psalms in the Psalter). You take breaks in the series to introduce a topical series. You could preach Psalms for fifteen weeks, spend four weeks on "Cultivating Endurance," and then return to fifteen weeks of the next fifteen Psalms. You could preach Matthew 1–4, turn to a series on "God at Your Job" for six to eight weeks, return to preach twelve weeks on the Sermon on the Mount, turn to another four-week topic series, and then return to Matthew 8–10 for six weeks. This will keep the anticipation of the return to the series in front of your people while they also enjoy other series you, as shepherd, might deem more immediate or needful.

In addressing the boredom associated with the lengthy *reading* of books, one might find Bonhoeffer's words helpful in addressing the lengthy *preaching* of books:

> Consecutive reading of Biblical books forces everyone who wants to hear to put himself, or to allow himself to be found, where God has acted once and for all for the salvation of men. We become part of what once took place for our salvation. Forgetting and losing ourselves, we, too, pass through the Red Sea, through the desert, across the Jordan into the promised land. With Israel we fall into doubt and unbelief and through punishment and repentance experience again God's help and faithfulness. All this is not mere reverie but holy, godly reality. We are torn out of our own existence and set down in the midst of the holy history of God on earth. There God dealt with us, and there He still deals with us, our needs and our sins, in judgment and grace. It is not that God is the

spectator and sharer of our present life, howsoever important that is; but rather that we are the reverent listeners and participants in God's action in the sacred story, the history of the Christ on earth. And only in so far as we are there, is God with us today also.[9]

Some places seem to be much easier for people to grasp and understand; this is only an appearance. There are no "easy" passages of Scripture. No one passage is easier to preach or hear. Passages are only more or less familiar—places we have encountered based on our cultural literacy, or having often heard them used with respect to Christian living.[10] As Bonhoeffer also notes,

If it is really true that it is hard for us, as adult Christians, to comprehend even a chapter of the Old Testament in sequence, then

---

9. Bonhoeffer, *Life Together*, 53–54.

10. Here, I disagree with Matt O'Reilly, who writes, "Certain genres of Scripture lend themselves more easily to whole-book preaching. In general, highly didactic texts are more straightforward and easier to explain. Such books will prove more fruitful in maintaining enthusiasm throughout the series on the part of preacher and congregation" (Matt O'Reilly, "Five Things You Need to Know About Preaching Through the Books of Scripture," https://www.preaching.com/articles/five-things-you-need-to-know-about-preaching-through-the-books-of-scripture). In Western cultures, we are more familiar with didactic literature because the Reformation bequeathed to us the preaching of Paul's epistles (including Hebrews, which was thought by many to be Pauline). So we are more familiar with didactic materials. Yet, again, there is nothing straightforward about what we read in Paul's literature (or other didactic material like the minor prophets, which O'Reilly counts among "didactic"). We simply do not spend the time working through the material in legal, poetical, narrative, and apocalyptic genres that we do in epistolary. As Daniel Darling admits, "Let's be honest. When those of us who are expositors talk about preaching verse-by-verse, we mean 'preaching verse by verse through the New Testament epistles because they are easier to divide'" (Daniel Darling, "How Expository Preaching Could Change the World," https://baptist21.com/uncategorized/2018/how-expository-preaching-could-change-the-world/). Moreover, the consistent butchering of supposedly straightforward didactic passages by preachers, such as Rom. 9; 1 Cor. 7; Eph. 3; Phil. 3:1–4:1; Phil. 1–25; Heb. 11; James 3; 1 John 1:1–2:2 and 2:3–17; Jude 1–25, in which sermons tend to be far from the writer's intended meaning in such passages, further argues that didactic is not as straightforward as it might seem to many.

this can only fill us with profound shame; what kind of testimony is that to our knowledge of the Scriptures and all our previous reading of them? If we were familiar with the substance of what we read we should be able to follow a chapter without difficulty, especially if we have an open Bible in our hands and participate in the reading. But, of course, we must admit that the Scriptures are still largely unknown to us. Can the realization of our fault, our ignorance of the Word of God, have any other consequence than that we should earnestly and faithfully retrieve what has been neglected? And should not ministers be the very first to get to work at this point?[11]

Psalm 23 may be the most-used verse for sharing during visits with infirmed members or at funerals. Based on its familiarity in comfort settings, and its place in our cultural literacy, it seems easier to understand than Psalm 63 or Psalm 89. Yet both Psalms 63 and 89 excel in their words of comfort. Psalm 63 ends with the affirmation, "But the king will rejoice in God; all who swear by God will glory in him, while the mouths of liars will be silenced" (v. 11). Similarly, near the beginning of Psalm 89, one reads, "I will declare that your love stands firm forever, that you have established your faithfulness in heaven itself" (v. 2). Both of these verses are packed with comforting truth—as much as Psalm 23:6: "Surely your goodness and love will follow me all the days of my life, and I will dwell in the house of the LORD forever." All three have words that hope confidently in the Lord to save the psalmist and your hearers.

Yet very few of our members will have memorized the eleven verses of Psalm 63; even less have memorized the fifty-two verses of Psalm 89! Thus, Psalm 23 will continue to seem easier to understand than psalms with which one is less familiar. Passages we think of as easy need as much attention as those that appear to be

---

11. Bonhoeffer, *Life Together*, 51–52.

"hard"—whether that is hard in terms of interpretation or application. If we think a passage is "easy," we may have missed some of the depth of what God is saying.

For example, "dwelling in the house of the Lord forever with the Lord's goodness and mercy present" has overtones of Exodus 34:6–7 and the Davidic covenant (2 Sam. 7), and might make an echo back to Psalm 25:8—the psalm immediately preceding it: "*Good* and upright is the Lord; therefore he instructs sinners in his ways." Surely, Psalm 23:6 points forward to John 10 and the Good Shepherd ministry of the Lord—the ministry that goes through the cross so that those who believe upon Christ might dwell with Him and the Father forever (see John 10:11, 15, 17, 18, 27). Psalm 23:6, then, speaks of the eternal ministry of the Lord to us as a Shepherd and our eternal relationship to Him as one of His sheep—a tender care/dependency relationship that continues through all eternity. Also, the "surely" speaks of the present eternal security of the sheep's salvation on the basis of the work of the Shepherd *alone*, just as the New Testament also sets forth that salvation is by grace alone through faith alone based on the work of Christ alone (see Acts 15:11; Rom. 5:15–17; Eph. 2:8–9; Titus 2:11; 3:7). The truth in this one verse makes this verse no easier to interpret or apply than Psalms 63:11 or 89:2! Familiarity with a verse is not the same as understanding the depths of the verse. The lack of familiarity of a verse or passage might lead one to think the verse is harder to understand simply because one cannot assume understanding of something with which one is not familiar.

## How to Preach through Books

Where, then, would be a good place to begin preaching through books of Scripture? I suggest you to start with a small and familiar book, like Jonah. Give people a taste of the series by working through an overview of the book in one message. Prep your people for the message by giving them a two- or three-week notice before you start the series, and invite them to read through Jonah ahead of the series. Also ask them to spend some time meditating on the Jonah typology in Matthew and/or Luke (Matt. 12:39–41; 16:14–17; Luke 11:29–32).

Maybe try preaching through Mark or a portion of Mark next. In this way, you will change testaments while continuing in narrative genre. You will introduce many people to the gospel story. You can cover a full series through the book in twelve weeks.[12] Again, invite your people to read Mark in full ahead of the series.

I would encourage you to attempt to preach through any two books of Scripture during some part of the next twelve months. I suspect that you will have an experience that will change your life, your preaching, and the lives of the people you are called to serve. You will be eager to hear the Lord speak to you in this way again, and your people might crave such preaching too.

Until you become used to preaching through books with regularity, here is a suggested method of study to prepare for exposition through books:

1. Prayerfully read through the entire book, asking the Spirit of God to reveal both the unifying idea of the book and gospel portrayals within the book.
2. In a notebook or journal, take notes on the book as you read. You will begin gathering sermon ideas almost immediately upon reading; you want a place to keep them.

---

12. For a study guide that works through the book in twelve units, see Dane C. Ortlund, *Mark: A 12-Week Study* (Wheaton, IL: Crossway, 2013).

As you are reading, journaling, and memorizing, observe human interest stories, illustrations, applications of obedience to or failure toward the main ideas you are developing as they come to mind.

3. Listen to sermons on the book and/or read other expositions of the book. Sermoncentral.com has archives of many book series.

4. Work through the book with your own study. Utilize a study guide. Read through commentaries, articles, and study Bibles written by and for women, and not simply those written by men, so that you will become attune to unique concerns women might have with various passages of Scripture.[13]

5. In addition to the most well-known commentary series, look at African and African American commentaries on your passages, including those found in the *Africa Bible Commentary*,[14] *The Africana Bible*,[15] *The Africa Study Bible*,[16] *The African Heritage Study Bible*,[17] and *The African American Devotional Bible*.[18]

13. Carole A. Newsome, Sharon H. Ringe, and Jacqueline E. Lapsley, eds., *Women's Bible Commentary*, 3rd. ed., rev. and updated (Louisville: Westminster John Knox Press, 2012). Catherine Clark Kroeger and Mary J. Evans, eds., *IVP Bible Commentary for Women* (Downers Grove, IL: IVP, 2002); Dorothy Kelley Patterson and Rhonda Harrington Kelley, eds., *Women's Evangelical Commentary: Old Testament* (Nashville: B&H Publishers, 2011).

14. Tokunboh Adeyemo, *Africa Bible Commentary: A One-Volume Commentary Written by 70 African Scholars*, 2nd. ed. (Grand Rapids: Zondervan, 2010).

15. Hugh R. Page Jr., et al., eds. *The Africana Bible: Reading Israel's Scriptures from Africa and the African Diaspora* (Minneapolis: Fortress Press, 2009).

16. *The Africa Study Bible* (Carol Stream, IL: Tyndale, 2016).

17. *The Original African Heritage Bible—KJV* (Valley Forge, PA: Judson Press, 2007).

18. *KJV-African American Devotional Bible* (Grand Rapids: Zondervan, 2007).

6. Outline the series as you intend to preach it and give each week's message a tentative title. Give a title to the series corresponding to the meaning of the whole book and what you want people to remember. As an option, you could follow the divisions of a short study guide through a biblical book and invite your people to utilize the study guide in their own personal or group study during the series.[19]

7. Think of songs that you would like to accompany each sermon and/or to give your music/worship leaders as they begin finding songs.

# CONCLUSION

After the postexilic generation of Judah rebuilt the temple, Ezra read the entire Law to them (Neh. 8). Nehemiah, the Levites, and others interpreted for them what they heard—not translating from one language to another but giving the sense of what the words meant (Neh. 8:8–9). They responded with weeping for hearing what they had missed and not obeyed. But Nehemiah and Ezra called for the day of the reading to be one of celebration (8:10–11).

Think of what they heard interpreted for them—not just verses about curses but about building parapets (Deut. 22:8) and planting one king of seed (22:9), about the future of the sons of Jacob twice, once in Genesis 49 in association with the hope of Shiloh and the lion of Judah, and in Deuteronomy 32 in connection with God as the Rock of the tribes of Israel. They also received words about testing the virginity of a wife (Deut. 22:13–21) and taking

---

19. I strongly recommend the Knowing the Bible series by Crossway. Several of these study guides also are available online as part of free courses through The Gospel Coalition: https://www.thegospelcoalition.org/course/knowing-Bible-mark/#week-1-overview.

a rebellious and gluttonous son to the elders for stoning (Deut. 21:18–21). Moreover, they heard words explaining the census that separated priests from those who could go to war (Num. 1), multiple times of keeping the Sabbath (Ex. 16:23–30; 20:8–11; 31:13–17; 35:2–3; Lev. 19:3, 30; 23:3; 26:2; Num. 15:32–36; Deut. 5:12–15), and multiple times of Moses's failure in the wilderness (Num. 20:10–13; 27:12–14; Deut. 1:37; 3:26–27; 32:48–52).

These words that caused grief as they revealed sin became for them words that were celebrated because they could hear God's voice with understanding and know that they were recipients of His blessing. As you preach through the Word of God, not avoiding the seemingly rough and harsh words and passages, your people too can weep over their sin as God's standards are revealed; they can rejoice as those who have received mercy though undeserving, and as those who are hearing the sense of the words of God as you walk them through the books of Scripture.

Similarly, the apostle Peter indicates that some of the apostle Paul's writings contain words hard to understand (2 Peter 3:15–16):

> Bear in mind that our Lord's patience means salvation, just as our dear brother Paul also wrote you with the wisdom that God gave him. He writes the same way in all his letters, speaking in them of these matters. His letters contain some things that are hard to understand, which ignorant and unstable people distort, as they do the other Scriptures, to their own destruction.

Yet the inclusion of these words indicates that the apostle Peter pursued trying to read "all [the] letters" of the apostle Paul available to him. The letters of Paul were important and authoritative to the *apostle* Peter and those to whom he was serving through his writing. Peter found Paul's writing important for the *lives* of the people he served. He reminded them that Paul's writing on the Lord's patience and salvation was both consistent with what Peter wrote, and that it was evident throughout Paul's writings (see Rom. 2:4, 7; 8:22; 9:25; 11:25; 1 Cor. 13:4; Eph. 2:21–22; Gal. 3:21–25; Col. 3:12–14; 1 Tim. 1:16), and it came by means of the wisdom of God. All of this Peter gathered as he *read* Paul—as he "beat importunately upon Paul"[20]—and he assumes that his own readers will gather the same in agreement. What they read and heard will be gathered by your hearers as you preach through the books containing the ideas to which the apostle points.

The breadth of God's truth for you to preach to your people, from both the Old and New Testaments, from law, narrative, poetry, prophecy, epistle, and apocalyptic—you can herald it in a manner that will make your people hunger to hear the consistency of God's voice through Scripture. Take your people through books regularly and let the Lord's voice arise from the pages of Scripture. You yourself will be shaped into godliness as you give the full witness of Christ to your people.

---

20. Martin Luther describes his reading of Paul in this manner in order to understand the doctrine of justification Paul taught. See John Piper, *Brothers, We Are Not Professionals: A Plea to Pastors for a Radical Ministry* (Nashville: B&H Publishing, 2013), 28–29.

# ACKNOWLEDGMENTS

In addition to my fellow contributors, this work comes to fruition because of yeoman efforts on the parts of many at Moody Publishers, including Siri Chammavanijakul, Drew Dyck, Kevin Emmert, Jeremy Slager, Connor Sterchi, and Karen Waddles. Special thanks goes to Paul Santhouse, VP of Publishing, and Randall Payleitner, Associate Publisher, for embracing the dream of this work and offering to help fulfill some of my passion for serving within the African American community. Thank you, too, to cover designer, Charles Brock.

My own thoughts about African American preaching and biblical exposition are shaped by hearing so many faithful expositors of my own hue during my earliest years of ministry. The names of such preachers include E. K. Bailey, William L. Banks, Ken Barney, Keith A. Battle, A. Michael Black, Ronald Crawford, Bernard Fuller, D. Lee Owens, Keith Reed, John Rhoades, Haywood Robinson III, T. L. Rogers, Terry D. Streeter, James Sturdivant, Patrick Walker, and Guy Williams. Some of those names are of preachers who now stand glorified in the very presence of our Lord Jesus. Even so, after almost three decades of ministry, I continue to stand on the shoulders of each of these men and in their debts in all the ministry that I do.

I am extremely grateful to Charlie Dates for pushing to make this work worthy of having "African American Tradition" in the title. You, Dr. Dates, are a gift to the body of Christ.

Many read early drafts of my chapters, including Pastor Larry Thompson of the Upper Room Worship Center, and Pastor Greg Wardlow of the Bradburn Memorial Bible Church. Thank you to everyone who made suggestions and gave affirmations of this work.

Finally, no work I do happens apart from the strong support and encouragement of my parents, Dr. and Mrs. Walter and Linda Redmond, my children—the Five Cs—Charis, Chloe, Candace, Calvin, and Codell, and the love of my life, Pamela Redmond.

Pam, my Autumn,of course this work, like all of my works, foremost I dedicate to you above all other finite beings. You are the most beautiful person the Lord ever has created. I love you and love being loved by you.

# A TREASURE TROVE OF
# SERMON ILLUSTRATIONS

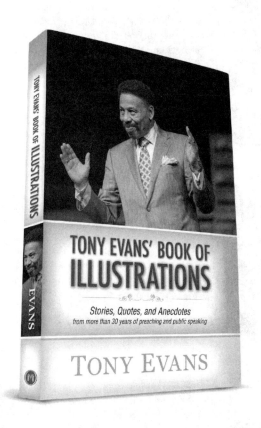

# TAKE YOUR PREACHING TO
# THE NEXT LEVEL

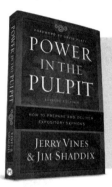
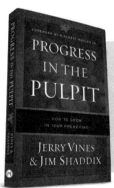